The WRONG SKIRT

THE QUEST
TO AVOID BAD CHOICES

BY

ROD DAVIS

Post Gutenberg™

AN IMPRINT OF
GLOBALEDADVANCEPRESS

Library of Congress Control Number: 2011920780
Davis, Floyd Rodney aka Rod Davis 1947 –
       The Wrong Skirt: The Quest To Avoid Bad Choices
       ISBN978-1-935434-55-9

       Subject Codes and Description:
       1: REL-012000: Religion - Christian Life - General
       2:REL-012070: Religion - Christian Life - Personal Growth
       3:REL-075000: Religion - Psychology of Religion

Cover Design by Barton Green

Published by
Post-Gutenberg Books™
An Imprint of GlobalEdAdvancePRESS
www.gea-books.com

Dedication

Who do you thank when there are so many whom God has used, and is still using, to impact my life with their wisdom and prayerful support? Nevertheless, I will try:

To my Lord and friend, Jesus, who taught me how to lose in order to win. There are no words to describe all you mean to me.

To my children, Jamey, Paula, Sarah, and my grandsons C.J. and Mad Max. I love you all very much. There could never be a prouder Dad.

Bob Lubell, a true friend who stood with me when others walked away.

Dr. Mark Hanby, you taught me to write with a rifle and not a shotgun. Mark, you're the one who told me, "Rod, you need to write a book."

Bart Green, my editor and long time friend. This book might not have happened if not for your dedication and hard work. Thanks buddy!

Robin Neil, you are a constant source of encouragement to me. No one could ask for a better friend.

And **Pastor Roy Cantrell,** you always believed in me. Your encouragement is priceless!

Contents

Introduction

FOLLOWING THE WRONG SKIRT

The Way That Seems Right

T hey will stand before God, look up and find themselves staring into the face of a stranger.

"There is a way that seems right to a man..."
(Proverbs 14: 12)

A s a small boy tagging along behind my mother through a large Chicago department store, my tiny eyes were opened to capacity as they darted from place to place attempting to take in this new world of shapes, lights, and colors. We passed through aisle after amazing aisle. Shelves were lined with an assortment of strange and beautiful objects. Mom's arms were filled with the spoils of her latest shopping conquest. She couldn't hold my hand, so I clung tightly to the hem of her red skirt as we went from floor to floor slipping in and out of aisles in a relentless search for that "real bargain".

My toddler-size attention span was reaching its limits when suddenly something amazing happened. Our safari through the merchandise jungle led us into a place of marvels and magic. I never thought such a world existed! TOY LAND!

"Mommy," I cried in excitement. "l-o-o-o-k-k-k!!!" My heart began to pound faster and faster! "Mahh-mee!!!" There was still no response. She had long ago entered into a feeding frenzy somewhere back in the lingerie department and my attempts at attracting her attention were lost in the foray. *Gosh! Couldn't she see all the neat stuff?! Miles and miles of... TOYS!*

I released my grip on her skirt for just a moment and tried to get a closer look. It was all too wonderful! After all, we're talking about millions of balls, tanks, plastic guns, toy soldiers and an assortment of curious looking gadgets that I had never seen before. *Had Santa come and no one told me?!* I certainly hoped not!

Suddenly, the throng of wild-eyed bargain hunters closed in around me and I was whisked away. Looking over one shoulder

I saw Toy Land quickly vanish behind the press. I struggled to glance over my other shoulder only to catch a fading glimmer of red from my mother's skirt.

I tried to push my way in her direction, but I was no match for the blitz of shoppers that was dragging me away. The time for panic had officially arrived. I waved my puny arms and shouted as loud as I could, but my cries of distress were shrouded in the hustle and bustle of a mega department store sale. I was desperately trying to push my way through the forest of legs, bobbing and weaving as I dodged swinging pocket books.

I was working my way around a lady with a posterior roughly the size of Rhode Island, when the crowd suddenly thinned. I could finally catch a faint glimpse of my mother's familiar red skirt moving further and further away. I strained with my last ounce of strength, until I found myself within grasp. Then leaping with hand extended, I caught a hand full of fabric in a *death grip* and held on tightly.

Once again I found myself being carried past columns of shinning merchandise and colorful signs that shouted, "Buy me!" But soon the excitement began to give way to exhaustion, and I was ready to call it a day. I just wanted to go home, crawl in my cozy bed, and forget this day ever happened: except for the part about Toy Land, of course.

My face felt like lead as I lifted it. "Mommy, I wanna go home... I'm tired!" I was waiting for my Mom's familiar voice to respond, when suddenly everything came to an abrupt halt and I plowed into her backside!

"Well, well... where did you come from?!" came a cheery reply from above. I looked up at the person towering over me and *found myself staring into the face of a total stranger!* I had grabbed the *wrong* red skirt! I had been following someone I thought was my mother all over that large department store while my real mom was frantically searching for me. There I was lost in a world of giants.

I was totally confused and frightened. If I had just held tightly to my mom's red shirt I wouldn't have been distracted by all the shinny toys. I wouldn't have been tempted to let go of Mom's skirt to get a closer look. I wouldn't have lost sight of her red skirt.

As Bill Shakespeare once said, "All's well that ends well." The nice lady, who for short time had me for a caboose, took me to the store manager. He made an announcement over the department store's PA system, "Attention please. Will the mother of a little boy, calling himself Rodney Davis, please come to the Managers Office." Soon Mom came to the office, swept me up in her arms, and I was joyfully reunited with her and all the world was right again.

Looking back I wonder how many of us who call ourselves Christians are like that lost little boy. We think we have a firm grip on the truth until we become distracted by the toys that the world and empty religion offers. We let go of the right skirt and get a death grip on the wrong shirt which drags us further and further away from God.

We let religious attitudes and the baseless traditional teachings of men lead us astray. Then while we're clinging to the wrong skirts, we make wrong decisions and soon we lose sight of God's plan for our lives.

The 18-Inch Deficit

One day Philip asked Jesus, "Lord, show us the Father."
Jesus seemed taken back at his appeal. "Don't you know *me*
Philip, even after I have been among you such a long time?"[1]
On another occasion Jesus made this startling declaration. "Not
everyone who calls me,' Lord, Lord,' will enter the kingdom of
heaven."[2] He then went on to say that there would be "many" who
professed to know him and would even claim to have performed
miracles in his name. However, Jesus' response to their boast is
most alarming! "... then I will tell them plainly, *I never knew you.
Away from me, you evildoers!*"[3] Why would Jesus say such a
thing to people such as these?

There is a way that seems right to a man,
but in the end it leads to death.
(Proverbs 14: 12)

What if we've fallen to the bottom of a well
Thinking we've risen to the top of a mountain
What if we're knocking at the gates of hell
Thinking we're heaven bound
What if we spend our lives thinking of ourselves
When we should have been thinking of each other
What if we reach up and touch the ground
To find we're living life upside down[4]

Countless numbers are going to miss heaven by 18
inches! This is the approximate distance between the head and the
heart.   Jesus said that there are *many* who mistakenly think that

everything is all right between them and God and that their place in Heaven is secured. They profess a faith of sorts in God and even claim to be Christians. They may lead fairly moral lives and regularly attend church. Yet, they're deceived.

Like that lost little boy they think they have a firm grip on God but they don't. Rather, they are holding tightly to something that *seems right.* They've made an intellectual ascent by accepting the historical Christ, but they have never made a commitment to his Lordship. *They have a death grip on the wrong skirt which is some mistaken concept of Christianity. However, when Jesus returns they will find that they were wrong—dead wrong!*

There were people like this in Jesus' day. The Scribes and the Pharisees[5] were the religious leaders in Judea. They knew more about the Bible and how to follow their religious code of conduct than anyone. Sadly, many looked to them for spiritual guidance. These spiritual leaders were certain that they knew God. Yet when Emmanuel, which means "God with us", was speaking to them face to face they didn't recognize him. "Who are you?" they asked.[6]

They had a firm grip on their own religious and philosophical worldview. They felt certain of their position. There was just one problem; they were holding on to the wrong skirt. The very thing that they were certain was drawing them closer to God, was in fact dragging them further and further away from him. *Their religion was, in reality, a death grip leading them to their doom.*

Today's churches are much the same. They're full of people who are clinging tightly to their certain concept of Christianity. Yet all too often, it's a passed down religious point

of view, rather than something they have come to know on a
personal basis. It's a *way which seems right*, but what is its end?
Do they personally know Jesus or are they merely trying to be
religious? Do they really know what it means to be born again, to
give yourself completely to Christ? If not, one day their life will
come to a screeching halt. They will stand before God, look up
and find themselves staring into the face of a stranger.

In John chapter 3 Jesus had a personal encounter with
one who was suffering from *The Wrong Skirt Effect*. Nicodemus
was a deeply devout Pharisee who enjoyed high standing in the
community and was a member of the Jewish equivalent of our
Supreme Court—the Sanhedrin. No one was more religious than
Nicodemus or loved and wanted to serve God more.

Yet Jesus looked him straight in the eye and said, "I tell
you the truth, no one can see the kingdom of God unless he is
born again."[7] His point was this, "Nicodemus, it doesn't matter
how religious you are or how righteous you think that your belief
system makes you. It's not good enough. You MUST be born
again!" In other words, "Nick ole buddy, you have a good strong
grip on *the wrong skirt,* and you're being carried down a path that
will ultimately lead to death!"

A Deadly Misconception

You, or someone you know, may be very much like
Nicodemus. You may consider yourself to be a decent, moral
sort. You may know something about the Bible. You may go to
church and perhaps give generously when the collection plate
passes by. You may actually teach Sunday School or even stand
behind a pulpit and delivered a sermon. However, if you've never

surrendered your life completely to the Lordship of Christ and truly repented[8] of your sins you're a victim of *The Wrong Skirt Effect*, and all of your religious hyperactivity means absolutely nothing! Being merely religious doesn't earn you brownie points with God and it certainly doesn't secure your place in Heaven.

Sadly, many are holding on with white knuckles to this deadly misconception. They continue to cling tightly to the wrong skirt. They are dragged through life thinking, or at best hoping, that everything is okay between them and God. The grim reality, however, is that they are lost and very far from the truth.

> *Again, if the trumpet does not sound a*
> *clear call, who will get ready for battle?*
> (1 Corinthians 14:8)

What has spawned all the confusion? Why are so many lost in a cloud of befuddlement? Why are our church pews cluttered with people suffering from *The Wrong Skirt Effect*? Is it possible that we, the church, are responsible? Could it be that the problem stems from the fact that much of the church has lost its focus? Were all the *wrong skirts* birth from the mixed messages that the world hears and sees from us? Has strife, division, and open hypocrisy diverted the attention of non-Christians from the truth? Is it us? Have we so muddied the Gospel[9] message that there doesn't seem to be a *clear call* anymore? In a word—*yes!*

Extremely Contagious

> *"So if the Son sets you free, you will be free indeed."* –Jesus
> (John.8:36)

What are some of the wrong skirts to which we cling? What are some of the traditional teachings of men that have caused much of the religious bigotry that many of us hold dear? Worse yet, what are we passing down to others? What are some of the skirts we offer to those around us? You see, this disease that so many suffer from is not only deadly it's extremely contagious.

"Be careful," Jesus said to them. *"Be on your guard against the yeast [teachings]of the Pharisees and Sadducees."* — Jesus (Matthew 16:6)

How can we rid ourselves of this destructive condition? What can we do to cut through all the religious rhetoric and offer true direction to those around us who don't know Jesus? We're going to take a look at wrong skirts, death grips, and the confusion plaguing the modern church. Then I will offer some suggestions on how we can be *free indeed* of *The Wrong Skirt Effect*.

1

THE 'COMFORT-ZONE' SKIRT

Changing Buses

Our choices, experiences, and decisions
are much like getting on a bus to go somewhere.

*"But He knows the way that I take; when He
has tested me, I will come forth as gold."*
(Job 23:10)

I n January of 1970, I completed my tour of duty in Vietnam and returned to the good ole U.S.A. After three weeks of well earned leave time, I kissed a weeping mom and a proud dad goodbye and flew off to Fort Hood, Texas. There I spent the last year and a half of my army career. During that time a pivotal event took place in my walk with the Lord. I was about to board a *bus* that was to take me on a strange and exciting new journey.

I was passing through a hallway at Company Headquarters heading back to my room, a paperback novel, and eventually bed. Being a typically goal oriented male, I wasn't paying too much attention to what was going on around me. In my mind's eye I was already lost in a snake-infested jungle with Tarzan the Ape Man, watching him clash with some villainous Arabs. Jane was in trouble! I needed to get back and help him rescue her from her latest dilemma.

I was almost out of the front door, and on my way to the darkest regions of Africa, when I brushed shoulders with someone coming in as I was going out. I had nearly made my escape across the parade field when he called out.

"Hey, wait up!"

His shout was almost lost in the sound of a close order drill passing nearby. "Idel-leaft... idle-leaft. Idle-leaft-hart-leaft... idel-leahft!! Two... three... four... " (civilian translation: "To the left... to the left-right-left... to the left!") A platoon of men, clad in neatly pressed fatigues, was rounding the end of Company Headquarters Building and was nearing the corner of the next building up. An E-7 (that's a Sergeant First Class for you civilians) dressed in khakis, with a crease in his pants that could be used to slice tomatoes, was barking out commands from underneath his Smokey-the-Bear hat in drill instructor lingo. "Column lee-aft!... huhh!!!" With that command line-by-line they made a precision left turn and then disappeared behind the building.

"Hey, Rod! Wait up!"

I finally heard him over the fading, *Left... hart... lefts*, of the now invisible platoon marching further away. I slowed my pace and turned to see who was hailing me. A tall sandy headed man with a broad smile was trotting my way. He was dressed in civvies (civilian clothes), which wasn't uncommon for a Friday afternoon. I came to a stop and allowed him to catch up.

"Hi! How-ya-doing?", he said, slightly out of breath.

"Great! How about you?" I was stalling for a name to go with the face. *Who is this guy!* I wondered. *I am so bad with names! I can usually remember faces, but names... rats! Who is he?* I felt like Winnie the Pooh sitting in his Thinking Place, "Think... Think! Think! Think! Think!" *Silly ole Rod.*

"You *do* remember me, don't you?" he asked. Boy, the pressure was really on now! I did as I usually do when facing a potential embracement.

My humor mode kicks in. I thought of the old joke about the armless man who was a bell ringer at a huge cathedral. He used his teeth to pull on the rope and ring the church bells. One day while crossing a busy intersection, he was struck by a '62 Plymouth and instantly killed!   As the crowd gathered, a pudgy lady in flared polyester slacks and sporting a three foot hair-do exclaimed, "Oh my *Gawed*! How *awww*-ful! Does anybody know who he is?!" A man wearing a pea green sport coat and a bad toupee adjusted his glasses and bent over to get a closer look at the twisted figure laying at his feet. He wrinkled his forehead, straightened himself back up and declared, "I don't think so, but his face rings a bell." (*Tah... Thump-Thump!*)

"Why, I'm Bob!" He said, seeming slightly offended.

"Of course... ah, Bob. Bob... ah ..." I was still trying to salvage the moment.

"You know me," said the face in question. *If I knew you I wouldn't be standing here with this "Duhhh!" look on my face!*

"Laselier... Bob Laselier!" he announced with just the slightest tinge of hurt in his voice.

"Yes, yes, I knew that... of course." I was still trying to keep my head above water. "How are you, Rob?"

"That's Bob." he repeated.

"Yeh, ah... that's what I said, Bob!... Bob. How are you... *Bob* ?"   Once the embarrassment subsided we shared some small talk, and then he told me why he chased me down. He was inviting me to a get-together for "a little fellowship and the Word" as he put it. I didn't have to think long and hard about that invitation. I had no Christian friends to speak of and was starving for some good ole down home fellowship. Bob went on to give me the where's and when's of the meeting. A friend of his would be picking us up that evening at six.

He parted with a "God bless you!" and went his way. I was overjoyed and filled with anticipation! So much so that I lost track of what I was doing and where I was going before my encounter with Bob. *What was it now?... Something to do with someone named Tarzan. Tarzan who? Oh well. Hey, I had better hurry and get ready!*

Oh yes, I was excited all right but I had no idea the impact this meeting was to have on me. I wasn't simply attending a small gathering of believers for some food and fellowship. Oh no! God was arranging a divine encounter, and I was the blessed target of a Holy Spirit set up! God had been putting his ducks in a row and, as usual, I was oblivious to it.

I didn't know then how quickly Bob and I would become dear friends. Furthermore, he was seemingly unaware of the fact that he was an instrument of God who was sent for a brief time to act as a middleman between me and my destiny. I had no idea of the life changing effect that encounter on a parade field at Fort Hood, Texas would have. You see, the meeting that Bob invited me to was hosted by the international ministry known as The Navigators.

I was instructed to meet Bob and his friend Dennis in the parking lot behind my barracks. They would be in a cream colored V.W. camper. "You know." Bob explained. "It's the kind with a fold out canopy? You know... on the side. You know... *Doncha?"* Oh no, pressure again... first faces, now automobiles! This reminded me of the story about a man with a mouse and a birdcage who went into a bar and ah... never mind. I quickly showered, put on my civilian duds, grabbed my Bible and hurried to the parking lot at the appointed time.

The Central Texas sun was covering the parking lot in an amber blanket as it began its slow decent into the horizon. I stood there bathed in its warmth and dazzled by its beauty. Surrounding me were dozens of cars fitting every description, with license plates representing nearly every state in the U.S. Each stood as a silent testimony to a young life that was separated from family and home in answer to America's call to service.

My wait was brief for soon a shiny V.W. camper, looking just as Bob described, pulled into the parking lot. In the front seat were two men who were smiling and waving. I recognized Bob in the passenger seat and returned the wave. They quickly found an empty slot and parked. The two of them were out of the van with right hands outstretched by the time I crossed the short distance to where they had parked.

Bob was the first to speak, "Hello Rod! I'd like you to meet Dennis Harvey." And with his introduction, I turned my attention toward a dark haired man with horn-rimmed glasses. He was slightly shorter than I and was sporting a blinding smile. He had a face full of teeth that would have made Jimmy Carter look like Walter Brennan. He looked somewhat like a 1955 Caddy with glasses. I had never seen so much grill work. In the next year or so that I spent with Dennis Harvey, I can count on one hand the number of times I saw him lose that winning smile.

"Hi, Rod, pleased to meet you!" I could tell he really was pleased.

"Nice to meet you too, Dennis." I responded. We climbed into the van and Dennis drove down the highway, chattering all the way. Our drive ended in a parking lot behind a large church in Killeen, Texas.

Killeen was a typical army town. It was filled with movie theaters, bars, clip joints, and shady characters of all kinds. The streets were lined with jewelry stores that had barkers standing out front on the sidewalks. They were constantly shouting at passing soldiers. "Come on in! You won't find a better deal in town! HEY! HEY! HEY! Come on in!" I hated to walk down those streets. Most of the people in this small town were decent folks, but there was an element of so called, "good loyal Americans" who were out to take everything they could from some poor unsuspecting soldier.

Dennis was still talking, smiling, and firing questions at me as we got out of the van. I wasn't sure what to make of him at first. He was a slight man of forty with a pleasant laid back disposition. He became involved with The Navigators while in the Air Force. When he was discharged from the military some months earlier, he moved in with local *Nav* rep Mel Duke and joined him in the ministry at Fort hood.

Meeting Dennis was a key strategic encounter in my spiritual journey. There are several men, most notably my father, who have left a vivid impression on my life. However, few men have made the impact that this gentle man from San Diego did. I can honestly say that knowing Dennis Harvey was a divine turning point in my life.

Catching the Bus

It was a gloomy Friday afternoon in January. The weather was typical of east Tennessee that time of year— cold and wet. I was approaching the end of a very long day and was beyond exhaustion. Lost in something of a half daze I sat in an old plastic chair made shinny by the countless number of teen-age backsides that buffed it over the years. All around me the walls of the band teacher's office were covered with plaques and framed certificates relating various tributes. Colorful music themed pictures of every size hung here and there.

One wall was all but covered by a large, nicely framed photo of smartly clad band members. Each uniformed figure grinned from ear to ear as they clutched their treasured instrument. Another large picture sat on the floor leaning against the wall behind the door; a dusty assemblage of hopeful, smiling faces who had long ago marched off into obscurity.

I had invested ten minutes staring blinding through a double class window into the colossal band room of an inner city high school. It was my second day as a substitute teacher. Today's assignment, sub for Miss Hill the band teacher. Being a *sub* is tantamount to being a glorified baby sitter and today was no exception. My task was to ride herd over 42 black teenagers for 50 minutes. Their mission was to seize every opportunity and use every means at their disposal to take advantage of this pudgy, simple looking, middle-aged, white guy.

It was another 40 minutes or so before my class came in. So, I sat in the office adjoining the band room and engaged myself in a conversation with the assistant band director. Mr. Gigliano was a portly man in his mid-30's who had a heart that matched his ample frame.

"This is an expensive flute." he said. He was leaning over a half dozen silver cylinders that were spread across the surface of his small desk. The flute had been damaged and he was attempting to repair it. "I told her father that she needed one, and he went out and got *this* one. I don't know where he got it... but it's expensive!"

A half dozen or so kids were sitting around a music stand talking at the top of their lungs and playing cards. One paced aimlessly around the band room while swinging his trumpet back and forth. From time to time he would raise it to his lips and blow some off-key tune known only to himself. The others didn't seem to mind the racket for they were a noise unto themselves. They just continued talking loudly, laughing, and shuffling cards about. Mr. Gigliano seemed oblivious to the clamor. Undaunted he continued working on the instrument.

"Most of these kids are good kids." he said. "They want to do the right thing. Many of them had mothers who used drugs or alcohol which caused them to be born with behavior problems."

I watched the activity in the band room as I listened to this gentle man speak. Another student stood up and began to roam about as well. He was circling the room and serenading no one but himself on his trombone.

"My wife tells me I care too much for these kids... I can't help it though." He put the last part of the flute together and blew it giving it a test run. "I just feel that there's a chance that I could say or do something that might make a difference in someone's life. That's what makes it all worthwhile… helping them make the *right* choices."

Mr. Gigliano reminisced fondly of past students who made *the right choices*, pressed on, and did something worthwhile with their lives. He was clearly thrilled at the aspect that he might have played the smallest role in their success. Mr. Gigliano countenance soon darkened, however, as he spoke of others who had every opportunity yet chose the lesser path. A tender young life was wasted because of bad choices that ultimately led to a dead-end.

As I listened I found my mind drifting back to choices I had made. Many of which, I am ashamed to say, were not the best of decisions. I thought about life, *my life in particular*, about choices and about... *buses*. Yes, buses. Our choices, experiences, and decisions are much like getting on a bus to go somewhere. I remembered many of these decisions, or *buses*, that brought me to where I am today. My thoughts seemed to scatter to the four winds and before long, I found myself adrift on a sea of memories.

I thought about family, friends, and other people God had put in my path. Some of which were like *bus drivers* and others like *ticket agents*. They were people who had touched my life in some significant way that helped carry me along life's journey. Then, as I continued my reflection, I considered the most important influence of all—Jesus. For without him I would have never survived the journey.

One's spiritual walk can be compared to a cross country bus trip. You get your ticket at one bus station, with the ticket comes you traveling information, naming your final destination. Then you board the bus. You do not, however, remain on that same bus for the entire trip. You *must* change buses and drivers at different terminals in order to get to where you're going. If you do not make the required changes, but remain on the same bus, you will never arrive at your final destination. Bob Laselier was a ticket agent. Dennis Harvey was a bus driver and The Navigators was a bus.

What is our final destination you may ask? There are actually many professing Christians who have no idea! Others believe that Heaven is our final destination. Many in this group act as if they simply received fire insurance when they came to Christ. They assume that they have climbed on board that Heaven bound bus and now they have an attitude that can be summed up in one statement, "I'll make it to Heaven someday, if I can just hang in there and try not to fall off the bus!"

This outlook is often reflected in the things they say. "Oh, you all pray for me that I might just make it through!" Or, "Yes brothers and sisters it's a hard ol' way, but remember that he who endures to the end shall be saved." "Oh... my mother-in-law is in the hospital at death's door. Pray that God will pull her through!"

My good friend Bob Lubell related this one to me. He was speaking in this church one night where a lady responded to a request for prayer needs by saying, "Oh... praise the Lord! You all just pray for me. Hallelujah... The devil's been beating me over the head all week long... bless his holy name!"

2

THE 'MONO' SKIRT

The Value Of A One-Sided Coin

... The US Mint does not offer a one-sided quarter and
the Gospel message does not present a one-sided Jesus!

"Therefore let all Israel be assured of this:
God has made this Jesus, whom you crucified,
both Lord and Christ. *"* — The Apostle Peter
(Acts 2:36)

A somewhat frail little man in a pale blue leisure suit walked into a bank. He looked around to see which line was the shortest and made a move toward line number two. Soon he found himself behind a little old lady with hair the same color as his suit. She was frantically digging through a suitcase size purse and mumbling to herself about someone named Wendell who "would lose his head if it wasn't fastened on!"

He was silently studying the tile on the ceiling, when he heard the teller say, "Next please. May I help you sir?" "Ah... yes," he said, stepping toward her window. "I need five dollars in quarters please. By the way, I would like quarters with only tails on them." "Excuse me sir?!" said the bewildered teller. "I... ah... thought you said you wanted quarters with... ah... no heads? Heh, heh! It's a little noisy in here today." "Yes mam, that's exactly what I said," he replied in a matter-of-fact tone. "You see, I'm not very fond of the heads on the coins. That particular picture of George Washington makes him look like a sissy! So please, give me quarters without the heads." The teller then flashed her bank-teller-smile that she learned at Bank Teller School and buzzed for the guard.

> *"... you will die in your sins; if you do not believe*
> *that I am the one I claim to be..."* — Jesus
> (John 8:24)

The Value of a One-sided Coin

There's a good chance that if you cruise your everyday novelty shop you'll find a one-sided coin, but you better not try to buy anything with it. You'll find that it's pretty worthless. Much of the Church has been offering something just as worthless—a one-sided Jesus! We've been preaching a noncommittal version of the Gospel that has failed to let those without Christ know that Jesus is a two-sided coin. He is Savior *and* he is LORD! Jesus is the one who liberates us out of sin's terrible bondage, but he's also the boss who is to be obeyed without question by those who follow him.

On his [Jesus] robe and on his thigh he has this name written: KING OF KINGS AND LORD OF LORDS. (Revelations 19:16)

The reason we're skipping the Lordship issue is simple. That side of the coin is not very popular. We don't want to make a commitment that may cost us something. Oh yes, we want the savior-side. Many of us may admit our need for a savior and we want him. That is as long as there's no obligation on our part. However, the US Mint does not offer a one-sided quarter and the Gospel message does not present a one-sided Jesus!

When we adopt this one-sided message it becomes a strictly needs-oriented Gospel. We present Jesus as the Savior who meets our needs but fail to declare him as the Lord who commands our obedience! We've laid aside the clarion call to repent and surrender to the lordship of Christ.

If anyone's name was not found written in the book of life, he was thrown into the lake of fire. (Relations 20:15)

"When the Son of Man comes in his glory, and all the angels with him, he will sit on his throne in heavenly glory. All the nations will be gathered before him, and he will separate the people one from another as a shepherd separates the sheep

*from the goats. He will put the sheep [his true servants] on his
right and the goats [those who never fully surrendered their
lives to him] on his left.* " — Jesus (Matthew 25:31-33)

The results of this ambiguous, watered-down, message
are that we now have a generation of goats who think that they
are sheep. They think that they are true followers of Christ but
they're not. This lame version of the Gospel has spawned a breed
of parishioners who have their name on the church roll but not in
the Lamb's Book of Life[10]. *Thus, they have a firm death grip on a
skirt that seems to be the right one but it will ultimately pull them
away from God and eventually drag them down to Hell!*
Yes our message should be, "Here's what Jesus will
do for you if you come to him." But it must also include the
unmistakable challenge "What will you do for Jesus?"

*"Therefore let all Israel be assured of this:
God has made this Jesus, whom you crucified,
both Lord and Christ."* — The Apostle Peter
(Acts 2:36)

Peter stood before the bewildered crowd that gathered
on the day of Pentecost[11] and proclaimed the uncompromising
Gospel![12] "Remember the man you crucified? This same man is
not only The Anointed One, the Savior, but God has also made
him LORD! Now... *what are you going to do about it?* " This kind
of undaunted message turns cities upside down and fans revival
flames across a nation. "He is Savior *and* LORD! Response
is mandatory!" It's little wonder that more than 3,000 people
responded and made Jesus their Lord that day.

The "What's in it for me?" Generation

This wimpy, milquetoast, message has spawned a generation of self-centered, powerless church members. It has created a people who have, to their open shame, relegated Jesus to the position of cosmic bellboy.

> ♪Jesus on the main line.
> Tell him what you want.
> Call him up and tell him what you want.♪
> (Traditional)

This "What's in it for me?" attitude is even reflected in the way that pastors and evangelists make their appeals for people to come forward and make a profession of faith in Christ. "Every head bowed... every eye closed. We don't want to embarrass *you*. Jesus is here to save *you*... to meet *your* needs. Just come to him and he will take *your* sins away and give *you* eternal life." It's true that he offers this and so much more than we can ask or imagine[13], but that's only one side of the coin! There is a commitment involved — the initial surrendering of one's will completely to God.

We've turned the Gospel into a message of, "Jesus has come into the world to personally serve you." However, it's a message that is quite to the contrary! Yes, indeed, Jesus came to the Earth to "seek and save that which was lost"[14], but he also brought with him the unyielding mandate to repent, take up your cross, and follow him!

Then he [Jesus] called the crowd to him along with his disciples and said: "If anyone would come after me, he must deny himself and take up his cross and follow me. For

whoever wants to save his life will lose it, but whoever loses
his life for me and for the gospel will save it."
(Mark 8:34-35)

Pressing the Lordship Issue

"The only freedom that man ever has is when
he becomes a slave to Jesus Christ."
— R. C. Sproul[15]

A Christian brother from England was overheard to say,
"The reason why you Yanks 'ave such difficulty with the Lordship
of Christ, is because you've never 'ad a bloomin' king!" Jesus is
the King of Kings and the Lord of Lords. He will accept nothing
less than our obedience. When a King speaks his subject listens.
When he commands our response is singular; we obey! That's
how one responds to a king— in reverential obedience. Yet, how
does the American Church answer this divine summons? They
reply with a resounding, "Here I am, Lord. Send... ah... *him.*"

They (the disciples) went out and preached
*that **people should repent.***
(Mark 6:12)

Jesus went into Galilee, proclaiming the good news of God.
"The time has come," he said. "The kingdom of God is near.
Repent and believe the good news!"
(Mark 1:14-15)

We must remember that "repent and believe the good
news [gospel]" is not a request. *It's a command from a King!*
Jesus didn't send out cute little embroidered invitations with the

words, "You are hereby cordially invited to repent and believe the Gospel. R.S.V.P." No! His voice rang out across the countryside. "The kingdom of God is near. *Now*, is the time for you to repent!"

I'm Slow but I Eventually Catch On

I remember a period in my ministry when I felt it necessary to soften my plea to my listeners to become a Christian. I reasoned that if I didn't make my appeal to come to Christ little less obtrusive, people would be scared away. I concluded that I would not get much of a response if I pressed the Lordship issue. Boy was I wrong, wrong... WRONG!

Every week I would preach my heart out, give an invitation, and then pace back and forth in front of the alter literally begging people to respond. Finally, after verse 62 of *Just as I Am,* I would dismiss the congregation, shake hands and listen to a few remarks like, "Good sermon, Pastor!" Then having concluded this weekly routine, everyone would hurry home to catch *The NFL Today.* The following Sunday we would begin the whole process again.

> *"Not everyone who says to me, 'Lord, Lord,' will enter the*
> *kingdom of heaven, but only he who does the will of my*
> *Father who is in heaven. **Many** will say to me on that day,*
> *'Lord, Lord, did we not prophesy in your name, and*
> *in your name drive out demons and perform many miracles?'*
> *Then I will tell them plainly, 'I never knew you.*
> *Away from me, you evildoers!'" — Jesus*
> (Matthew 7:22-23)

Much to my shame I didn't realize that I was offering my congregation a worthless one-sided coin. Subsequently, most of the very few who did respond did not understand the commitment involved in receiving salvation. Thus, they were joining the ranks of the *many* Jesus spoke of who are the victims of *The Wrong Skirt Effect*.

America Needs a King!

When he [Jesus] saw the crowds, he had compassion on them,
because they were harassed and helpless,
like sheep without a shepherd.
(Matthew 9:36)

When you tell others about Jesus and the salvation he offers, how do you present your message? Perhaps you do it much the way I did. You're afraid that you might be labeled a radical or maybe you're concerned about scaring people away with the lordship message. The truth, however, is quite to the contrary. The world is devoid of any true direction and its people are begging to be led. Jesus saw them as harassed and helpless, sheep without a shepherd. People are desperate for something to believe in, for *someone* to believe in.

Human nature thrives on a challenge. Just look around you. You'll see example after example of people responding to challenges of all kinds. Climb the highest mountain, dive in the deepest sea, eat the most hot-dogs, become the champion at something and so forth. So, why not give them the greatest challenge ever offered to a lost, shepherdless, race? "Come, follow me!"

"I believe young people are indifferent to the church today, not because the church has required too much of them, but because it has demanded so little." — Mort Crim[16]

Millions are familiar with the best seller book, "The Purpose Driven Life (2002) written by Christian author Rick Warren and published by Zondervan. The book has been on the *New York Times* Best Seller list for advice books for one of the longest periods in history while also topping the *Wall Street Journal* best seller charts as well as *Publishers Weekly* charts with over 30 million copies sold by 2007"[17] It's popularity is an example of what I saying.

The world is filled with a restless people on an unending quest. Not only are we looking for a savior to replace our feelings of hopelessness. *We want a life with a purpose.* We're looking for someone to follow. If you don't believe me just read a few of the current magazines or do some channel surfing on the ol' idiot box. It won't take long for you to find an example of some poor misguided soul who has left family and friends to follow some pseudo-messiah.

When I say to a wicked man, 'You will surely die,' and you do not warn him or speak out to dissuade him from his evil ways in order to save his life, that wicked man will die for his sin, and **I will hold you accountable for his blood.** (Ezekiel 3:18)

People need a king. Souls all over the world are crying out for a leader. If the Church doesn't offer one someone else will. There's always a Jim Jones or a David Koresh waiting in the wings ready to usurp the position that rightly belongs to Christ. It's up to us, his church, to present to the lost with the true and living Lord. We need to offer them a *two*-sided coin and make it very clear that salvation is dependent on their commitment. If we don't do this God will hold us accountable. We *must* preach the whole of the Gospel! Jesus is Savior and Lord! It's a packaged deal. *You can't have one without the other.*

Tolerating a Phony Gospel

As stated earlier, we're living in the "What's in it for me?" generation and the American church, at large, has tailored the Gospel message to fit into that philosophy. "Leave out the Lordship thing. Yeah, Yeah! That's the ticket! We can get more people to come to church if we do that. Yeah! Let's have a gospel singing. Yeah!... once a month. Yeah... a singing! That always pulls 'em in. Yeah... that's the ticket. Drop that ol' lordship thing! Yeah... that's the ticket." [18]

The sad result of such an attitude is clearly evident. Our churches consist largely of people who have never experienced real salvation. They continue to cling to a skirt which is "a way that seems right", but in actuality, it is a *wrong skirt* disguised as truth.

For if someone comes to you and preaches a Jesus other than the Jesus we preached,... you put up with it easily enough.
(2 Corinthians 11:4)

It would seem that this has been a long-standing problem that goes back to the days of the early church. Paul had to deal with those who were presenting a distorted gospel. The

contemporary western church has preached this wimpy message
for so long that we don't recognize it as counterfeit. We've grown
accustomed to the mundane and, like the Corinthians, have
learned to *put up with it easily.*

What a shame that we should exchange the glory of
serving the risen LORD for a cheap, synthetic, version of Jesus.
Paul takes this theme a step further and uses some of the strongest
language in the Bible.

*But even if we or an angel from heaven
should preach a gospel other than the one we preached to you,*
let him be eternally condemned!
(Galatians 1:8)

God is serious about his Gospel! Shouldn't the Church
be as well? Too much is at stake! Countless numbers of men,
women, and teens are seeking answers to life's perplexing
problems. They've grabbed every skirt that's come along and now
their world is in a tailspin. They've become disillusioned and have
lost all reason to hope that anything will change for the better. Our
cities are overflowing with desperate and lonely people who have
just given up on life. We've got to reach them with the truth!

"Who ya gonna Call?"

*And how can they believe in the one of whom
they have not heard? And how can they hear
without someone preaching to them?*
(Romans 10:14)

"America has more unchurched people than the entire
population of all but 11 of the 194 nations." — George Barna[19]

The question set before us is clear. Who is responsible, or dare I say *accountable,* for the presentation of this truth? Who are the lost masses looking to for this truth? Where are these people going to turn for help? To whom will they go for direction? Who's going to show them the *true* way? *Who ya gonna call?* No, it's not The Ghost Busters. They're looking to you! That's right... *YOU!* You, my fellow follower of Christ, are the only one they can depend on to give them the legitimate Gospel, rather than some one-sided version. They're waiting for you to present them with the good news. It's up to you and me to show them the way.

"I am the way and the truth and the life.
No one comes to the Father except through me." — Jesus
(John 14:6)

Imagine that you live in this large house. Now, everyone you know lives there — family, friends, co-workers, neighbors, banker, mail carrier, school mate, the person setting on the next seat on the bus, and so forth. Everyone that you encounter in your circle of activities lives in your house. The problem is that your house is engulfed in flames and is quickly burning down around all of you. There's only one exit out of this inferno and *you* know where it is, or rather *who* it is. Jesus is the door—the way out. Without you to point the way they will be trapped. *Only you* can lead them to The Door and show them the way out before it's eternally too late.

"Shout it aloud, do not hold back. Raise your voice like a trumpet.
Declare to my people their rebellion and to the house of Jacob
their sins." — God (Isaiah 58:1)

The responsibility to warn them lies squarely on our shoulders. They need us. How will they know unless we tell them? We must tell them that their hope lies in one direction only; that is in the complete surrender to Jesus as their Savior *and* their LORD. If we don't tell them clearly, God will hold us accountable for their blood.

"When sinners are careless and stupid, and sinking into hell unconcerned, it is time the church should bestir themselves. It is as much the duty of the church to awake, as it is for the firemen to awake when a fire breaks out in the night in a great city. The church ought to put out the fires of hell which are laying hold of the wicked. Sleep! Should the firemen sleep, and let the whole city burn down, what would be thought of such firemen? And yet their guilt would not compare with the guilt of Christians who sleep while sinners around them are sinking stupid into the fires of hell."

— Charles Fenny[20]

3

THE 'DISGUISED' SKIRT

Religion vs Relationship

It has a firm death grip on the throats of too many of our churches and is squeezing the very life out of them.

"They worship me in vain; their teachings are but rules taught by men." — Jesus (Matthew 15:9)

S ome years ago I spent a few weeks residing at my good friend Dough Mayfield's house. It was an old, somewhat dilapidated, two story structure that stood alone on a large farm as it had done for well over one hundred years. The house had been vacant for several months and was primarily used for storage. However, it had a functioning kitchen and bathroom and served well as my temporary home while I was between jobs.

Aside from the kitchen and bathroom, the only other accessible room was a bedroom upstairs. To get to it you had to work your way through a living room cluttered with boxes and unused furniture. Once you managed that room, you then stepped into the kitchen, hung a left, and entered the master bedroom at the other side of the kitchen. It too was stacked to the ceiling with more boxes and furniture.

Just inside this doorway and immediately on the left was a door. Behind this narrow door was an even narrower 'L' shaped stairway. This was the only access to the small bedroom upstairs where I spent my nights.

I hadn't been there long when I realized that I wasn't the only one living in that dusty, old house. During the daylight hours things seemed fairly quiet, but when the sun disappeared and darkness rolled in, that old house came alive. At night, as I lay in bed, I could hear the faint intermittent sound of movement downstairs. Sometimes it would be loud enough to rule out any question as to whether or not I was just hearing things. At other times it was difficult to distinguish between what was my imagination and what was real but I could undoubtedly hear... *something.*

At night I would lie very still, almost holding my breath, listening... carefully listening to what seemed to be the rustling of dozens of tiny feet. Each night that unnerving sound would come closer and closer to my bedroom. Louder and louder, closer and closer it would come, as though my roommates were gradually gathering up the courage to investigate the new squatter.

Then one night, I was startled awake by a racket that was louder than what I had grown accustomed to. Something much larger was responsible for this noise. There it was again! I felt my body tense and my nervous system go on overload. What was that?! This sound was not coming from downstairs. It was closer, much closer! As I lay there, surrounded by thick darkness, I could hear it plainly—the sound of something moving... IN MY ROOM!

Silently, and oh so slowly, I rolled over stretching my hand out into the blackness and found the lamp. *Click!* Blinding light flooded the room! I bolted upright in the bed! A furry shape went speeding across the floor! My eyes, now adjusting to the sudden glare, caught a sure glimpse of the fleeing intruder.

It was a rat! A *BIG* rat! It was like the ones I saw in Vietnam; such as the huge one that woke me up one night crawling across my legs. Oh yes, I had seen this kind before. There was no mistaking it. This is what we call here in east Tennessee, a gopher rat; the kind that grows large, mean, and ugly. I HATE RATS! And I sure didn't feel warm and safe as I watched his long snake-like tail disappearing down the stairs.

Like I said I deeply and sincerely hate rats! To be perfectly honest, the reason I hate them is because they terrify me! (Don't laugh! I bet they give you a few goose bumps too.) They frighten me and therefore, I hate everything about them—their long snouts, beady eyes, and long skinny tails. I can't stand the little disease-infested vermin! So, the next morning I set into motion...*Operation Rat*.

I rummaged about the house and found several rattraps. I then proceeded to spread them around the kitchen, putting them in the cupboards, under the sink, and behind appliances; anyplace I thought a rat might use for a hideout. After careful consideration, I thought it best not to put any in my bedroom. I didn't want any painful surprises to greet me on one of my *midnight nature walks*. Consequently, to be on the safe side, the traps were confined to the downstairs area.

Almost daily I would come home and find the lifeless corpse of some lesser rodent caught in one of my traps but never the big guy. Oh no, not Cujo Rat! He was older and wiser than his smaller comrades. He was too smart to be caught that easily. Cujo would somehow manage again and again to evade my traps. Then when nightfall came, and I thought myself to be safe and sound in my bed, he would pay me a little visit.

I would be settled in and just about to doze off when I would hear Cujo scurrying about. He would be scratching around underneath my bed, sticking his cold black snout down in my shoes, and leaving his little lumpy *calling cards* everywhere. I knew that he was toying with me. Some nights if I listened hard enough, I could swear that I heard the faint sound of snickering coming from a shadowy corner in my room and a small ratty voice whispering, "You got the others but you'll never get me. Heh-heh-heh!"

It was psychological warfare and Cujo was winning. Every night he would silently creep up my stairs and begin his campaign of harassment. I would lie there as quite as a mouse, (ah … *sorry!*) listening for the slightest sound of small, shuffling feet. I knew he was lurking there in the darkness, spying on me, and waiting for me to go to sleep. Then when I couldn't take the waiting any longer, I would shout, "HEY!" at the top of my lungs. "Get outta here you filthy varmint!" And with that, I could hear him high tail it across the floor and dash down the stairs.

I wasn't sure at the time as to why Cujo came upstairs every night. There was no food or any other lure there to entice him. It was just little ol' me up there, lying in my bed, trying to sleep. As I look back on that experience I may have come up with an explanation. *I* was the lure! *I* was the only possible attraction. Perhaps he viewed me as his nemesis. Peter Pan had Captain Hook, Moby Dick had Captain Ahab, and Jaws had Quint. Cujo had me. After all, I had sent most of his furry little friends to that big sewer in the sky. Perhaps inside that small ratty brain of his he was secretly plotting some sort of revenge.

Whatever the case, I knew someday we would meet face to face. We would have our showdown! It didn't take long for that day to arrive. The *close encounter of the rat kind* occurred late one dark and foreboding night.

I was returning from church and was eager to put an end to a long, tiring day. I was exhausted. All I could think about was getting into bed and going to sleep. Cujo and his pack of rodents was the farthest thing from my mind. I parked my car, got out and locked the doors. Yawning and stretching I look at lightning flashing in the distance, lighting up the darkened sky. A rumble soon followed announcing that the advancing storm would arrive in a matter of minutes. "It's going to be a loud night." I groaned.

I climbed the porch steps and entered the front door. I sleepily made my way through the maze of furniture and cartons in the pitch-black living room and then passed through the kitchen. I turned on the light in the master bedroom and found the door leading to the bedroom upstairs. Opening the door, I reached inside and turned on the light switch. The upstairs bedroom lit up brilliantly.

I was starting up the steps when suddenly; I heard what sounded like a small pony galloping across the floor. For an instant I couldn't tell where it was coming from. The sound reverberated off the walls of that narrow stairway and cascaded all around me. Two more quick steps got me around the 'L' and eye level with the bedroom floor.

I froze! Charging full speed toward me was the source of all the commotion! The showdown had come at last! I had finally met the enemy and the enemy was a terror stricken rat! Cujo was desperate to make his escape, and I was the unwitting barrier who blocked his way. He was suddenly faced with a choice—go through me or become trapped. He chose me!

It happened so quickly I didn't have time to think. Cujo lunged right at my nose! At first panic gripped my heart and I couldn't move! The bitter taste of fear rose up in my throat!

Down the stairs he leaped, scurrying about my feet! "Ah-h-h-h!!!" I screamed and started dancing up and down like a man with his shoes on fire. Yes, I was dancing but I wasn't in the Spirit. I also had a few choice words but, I'm sorry to say, I wasn't speaking in tongues or prophesying.

Through my legs and out the bedroom door he flew like he was fired out of a cannon! Before I knew it Cujo was gone as quickly as he appeared. I never saw or heard from him again. As far as I know he's still running. I staggered over to my bed and plopped down. There I sat breathing into a paper bag and waiting for my heart to start beating again.

A Lesson from a Rat

Well, it was over. I suppose I fared much better than Quint did with Jaws and I was no worse for the experience. That ordeal did, in fact, teach me something. Over the years since, I learned to draw some interesting parallels between rats and a lot of religious folks I know. *They both prefer the dark and can be uncommonly vicious when cornered.*

Religious Rat — the combination of two words:
Religious (ri lij' es) *adj.* and Rat (rat) *n.*

1. one whose religious value system and practices take precedence over truth and love for others.
2. one who prefers the darkness rather than the light.
3. one who values dogma over a relationship with God and with other believers.

You couldn't sling a dead cat without hitting one. No matter where you turn you'll inevitably run into at least one. "What is that?" you ask. I'm glad you asked. It's a religious person, of course. They're everywhere. They're like flies in a landfill, too numerous to count. You'll find them in the mall, at your favorite restaurant, at your place of business, at the YMCA, in your local bar, and at your next family reunion. Why, you might even set right next to one at church on Sunday! As a matter of fact, there's a very good chance that you saw one this morning staring back at you from your bathroom mirror!

God is not religious — *he's relational.*

I freely admit that I have a certain disdain for empty, bogus, religion. Allow me to explain. Often I'm asked by someone who recognizes that there's something spiritual about me, "Are you religious?" My response is simple and to the point. "NO! Hun-ah! No sir... not me! *God forbid!*" And with my reply I extend both hands with one forefinger resting on the top of the other forming the sign of a cross, as if to ward off a vampire. "No, no, no! Not me!"

It's great fun watching the responses I receive. They are frequently humorous and always marked with confusion. The conversation usually goes something like this:

"I don't understand... you... ah... act religious!"

"Oh pah-leezee! Don't insult me like that!"

"Now wait a minute! You go to church don't you?" his confusion growing.

"As often as I can"

"You're always reading the Bible aren't you?"

"Well, not always... I... I need to spend more time in *The Word* than I do, but I do read as..."

"Now, hold the phone!" he says in a *gotcha* tone. "I hear you talking about Jesus and singing about Jesus all the time. You drive me nuts! That's practically all I hear from you! Jesus this and Jesus that! Huh? And you say you're *not* religious?!"

"That's ri-i-i-ight!" I sing back to him. "And what you just said proves it."

His bewilderment has now given full sway to curiosity. My friend doesn't realize it yet but he is the target of a Holy Spirit set up!

"I... I don't understand. Explain yourself." And with that request I begin to present him with the Good News about Jesus. This *religion denial ploy* has become one of my favorite tools for sharing Jesus with others.

Let's be honest with one another, shall we? After all there's just the two of us. So, why play "Button, button, who's got the button?" Or in this case, *"Who's got the religious rat?"* I'll go first. Yes, I admit it. It saddens me to say that I have one or two of those little life-sapping varmints scratching around in the walls of my spiritual house. I've been trying to capture them for years and a... oh... *O.K!!* There's probably a few more scurrying about of which I'm not yet aware. However, I sincerely want to be rid of them all... *honest!*

Religion vs. Relationship

Webster's New World Dictionary defines the word *religious* as describing one who *believes in or supports a religion* or who *is concerned with religion*.[21] What's in your heart? Is there a religious rat living there? Jesus said that it's not difficult to tell. All one has to do is simply listen. Just listen to what a person says. Take your average church member for instance. Listen to what he talks about and you'll find out. It won't take long to discover if he has a *relationship* or a just a *religion*.

> *"The good man brings good things out of*
> *the good stored up in his heart,*
> *and the evil man brings evil things out of*

the evil stored up in his heart.
For out of the overflow of his heart his mouth speaks. "

— Jesus (Luke 6:45)

Consider a person who is merely religious. Their conversation solely centers on things of a religious nature, such as church activities, religious personalities, and so forth. Their focus lies purely within the framework of what their church, or their particular denomination, teaches and does. Therefore, those Christians who are not a part of their particular religious infrastructure are often viewed as "outsiders". They are poor misguided second-class saints rather than brothers and sisters in the Lord.

We are from God, and whoever knows God listens to us; but whoever is not from God does not listen to us. **This is how we recognize the Spirit of truth and the spirit of falsehood.** *Dear friends, let us* **love one another**, *for love comes from God.* **Everyone who loves has been born of God and knows God.** *Whoever does not love does not know God, because God is love. This is how God showed his love among us: He sent his one and only Son into the world that we might live through him. This is love: not that we loved God, but that he loved us and sent his Son as an atoning sacrifice for our sins. Dear friends, since God so loved us, we also ought to love one another.* — (1 John 4:6-11)

These *outsiders* are then routinely judged unfit by the religious crowd or at best considered to be inferior citizens of the Kingdom of God. "After all, they don't believe like us or do things the way we do them." This spiritual bigotry is entirely based on the fact that these *second-class Christians* are not affiliated with their particular *rat pack* or church denomination. Therefore, they are frequently spoken ill of by these good ol' religious folks and on occasion even treated with downright unkindness. *This elitist mindset is by far one of the most disgraceful behaviors displayed by the religious crowd!*

> *To fear the LORD is to hate evil;* **I hate pride and arrogance**, *evil behavior and perverse speech.* (Proverbs 8:13)

Now someone with a relationship with God, rather than empty religion, acts very differently. Their conversation is light years ahead of the religious crowd. Why? Elementary, my dear Watson. Much like the heavenly host in the scripture below, those with a *relationship* have a point of reference that falls squarely on the person of Jesus. *He, not their religious dogma, is the center of their lives.*

Heaven's Focus

> *Then I looked and heard the voice of many angels, numbering thousands upon thousands, and ten thousand times ten thousand. They encircled the throne and the living creatures and the elders. In a loud voice they sang: "Worthy is the Lamb, who was slain, to receive power and wealth and wisdom and strength and honor and glory and praise!" Then I heard every creature in heaven and on earth and under the earth and on the sea, and all that is in them, singing: "To him who sits on the throne and to the Lamb be praise and honor and glory and power, forever and ever!" The four living creatures said, "Amen," and the elders fell down and worshiped.* (Revelations. 5:11-14)

While imprisoned on the Island of Patmos[22], the Apostle John was privileged to see what few had seen before. He heard things that no human ear had heard before. John found himself transported from that tiny island to a place of such unimagined radiance and beauty that it overwhelmed all of his senses. Lost in total amazement he watched Heaven itself unfold before him. His heart swelled within his breast as he got a glimpse of the glory within.

What did John see as he peered into eternity? Many mysterious images paraded before him. He beheld things too extraordinary to describe in anyway other than celestial terms. Yet the one sight that impacted John the most was seeing the Lord Jesus surrounded by legions of worshiping saints, angels, and strange creatures that almost defied description, all caught up in worship of him.

He saw Jesus, the Lamb of God, being continually exalted and magnified by all who beheld him. The whole of the heavenly hosts was preoccupied with Jesus. John heard our Lord proclaimed to be worthy of all praise and honor! *He saw Jesus as the focal point of Heaven.* Indeed, those who have much more than religion *will be identified by their preoccupation with The Lamb as well.*

What's more, true *Jesus-lovers* will feel drawn to others like themselves. Not in the sense of a church or denominational affiliation, but rather, they are drawn to those who have a similar passion for their Lord. It does not matter in the least to *Jesus-lovers* where one attends church. The bond they share has little to do with *what* they belong to as it does with *whom* they belong to.

Have I flushed out any familiar religious rats in your life
yet? No? Keep going, I'm working on it.

Religious Exclusivity and Revelation Evasion

> *"They worship me in vain; their teachings are but*
> *rules taught by men."* — Jesus (Matthew 15:9)

The merely religious person believes that their particular
group, movement, church, or denomination has the market
cornered on truth. They consider every other professing Christian
an outsider who is devoid of the real truth. For those who follow
a bogus religion the major bulk of their theological base rests
solely within the framework of what their church or denomination
teaches.

This attitude is manifested in phrases like, *"That's not
Baptist!"* *"That's not Church of God!"* *"That's not Methodist!"*
or *"That's not Lutheran, Catholic,* and so forth." Incredibly,
they may even question some of the practices of their very
own beloved organization and even criticize one another, but
they would never question the teaching of their church or
denomination.

According to Webster the word *religion* comes from
an old French word meaning *to bind or to hold back.* Religious
rats resist theological expansion. They do *not* want to push the
spiritual envelope. They're in their comfort zone and do not want
their doctrinal boundaries challenged. They suffer from a terminal
case of *Revelation Evasion.* God help anyone who presses beyond
their limited revelation and questions their traditional teachings!

The sign posted on the front lawn of their church,

labeling their particular denomination or movement affiliation, are really *Stop Signs* that call a halt to proceeding beyond their particular belief system and practices. *If what someone has to teach or preach is not sanctioned by Cleveland TN, Nashville, Ft. Worth, Andersonville, Tulsa, Rome, or some other Mecca of Christendom, just forget it! They don't want to hear it!* After all when you've conquered that final spiritual frontier of Biblical revelation and have ascended to the ultimate plateau of truth, why go any further? Besides, what can some trouble making *outsider* teach one of such an elevated state of illumination anyway?

> *Jesus replied, "And why do you break the command of God for the sake of your tradition?... you nullify the word of God by your tradition that you have handed down. And you do many things like that."* — Jesus (Matthew 15:3&13)

I am firmly convinced that all doctrine *must* be subject to scriptural scrutiny. *All doctrine, no matter how cherished, must stand the test of The Word of God. If one's teachings are not clearly taught in Holy Scripture, by all means, let's put that little truth-choking doctrine out of its misery. For it's rooted deeply in baseless traditions of man and not God's WORD.*

Indeed, let's turn on all the lights! Let's flush out all of the religious rats lurking in the dark corners of our lives. Dismiss any teaching or tradition that would dictate limits on personal revelation. Abandon any doctrine or tradition that would ensnare you, cause you to forbid change, and keep you from going deeper into your relationship with God! In other words, *turn loose of that skirt!*

A Lesson from Nature

It's a law of nature that *when something stops growing it starts dying.* Growth means change. We must change or die! How can one who is merely finite arrive at such a colossal assumption? That is to insist that *their* church/denomination, also consisting of finite people, has arrived at a point of complete enlightenment? Therefore, change is out of the question. God forgive our arrogance!

I'm not trying to be intentionally offensive. Please, forgive me if you feel that I am. I try to be someone who expresses a certain measure of kindness and patience toward others who call themselves Christians. *It's just that I almost lose it when dealing with religious zealots who are more interested in preserving their hand-me-down belief system than they are in discovering the truth.*

When I see someone waving around little pet doctrines that have little or no scriptural basis, but rather have their roots deeply embedded in the traditions of men, I see red! (More about this in chapter four)

Squaring Off with Religious Rats

Sadly, this sort of blind adherence to ungrounded dogma leads one further and further into error. A man I used to know was a textbook example of this. He had some of the most outrageous views imaginable. "You know, I gotta watch who I get around... 'cause if I get next to somebody who's sick, their sickness will leave them and come on me... It's a gift that God... ah... God... ah... ah... *AH-CHOO!!* (Sniff)... gave me."

Everyday, just when I thought I had heard it all, he would come up with some other outrageous notion. "You know, it's a sin for women to wear pants." he volunteered one day. "Oh, really? Who says that?" I questioned. "Why... the Bible... the Bible says it! (Sniff)" he offered.

To that I gave my traditional response to extra-biblical homilies. "Chapter... verse, please!" "Why... ah... it's in there!" he said. "Chapter... verse, please!" I repeated. His complexion changed to a deep amber as he shifted his weight from foot to foot, looking like a trapped animal (or rat) looking for an escape.

"CHAP... TER... VERSE... PLEASEEE!!!" I slowly pronounced each syllable, in a *read-my-lips* fashion. I spoke softly and calmly but gave no quarter. I did not intend to offend him. I was just fed up with his constant dribble and was determined to have him put up or shut up!

His reaction was typical of all *religious rats*. Like my old adversary Cujo, a rat runs freely in the dark but will dart about seeking a place to hide when surprised by a sudden light. If he can find no escape, he will fight you with ferocity well beyond his size.

Thus it is with most religious folks. They move best in the dark, but shine the light of truth on them and they'll panic. Corner them and they will angrily attack the source of their discomfort. So it was with this man.

He went ballistic! "I... ah... it's... well... it's... IT'S IN THERE *SOMEWHERE*!!!" he shouted and stormed away mumbling to himself.

> *"While I am in the world, I am the light of the world."*
> — Jesus (John.9:5)

Jesus stood toe to toe with the religious rats of his day. He was radiant light bursting forth in their dark world of religious deception and man-made traditions. When he cornered them with the truth they savagely attacked him. Finally, in the greatest act of high treason the world has ever known, they butchered the King of Glory and nailed him on a cross.

Thus are the ways of religious rats. Because they feared the light, the religious leaders instituted the persecution against the early church. It wasn't the Roman government that was the first to shed Christian blood. It was highly respected *religious* folks like the ones who crucified the Lord! Yes, religious folks... much like you and I.

Jesus answered, "I am the way and the truth and the life. No one comes to the Father except through me." (John 14:6)

Take warning, my friend! *We must not let a bogus religious spirit blind us to the religious rats lurking in the dark recesses of our heart, lest we too find ourselves crucifying the truth in order to protect our traditions.*

Religion elitism has always been the most cunning and powerful opposition facing a move of God! Today it remains the leading hindrance to the American church's ability to work together to reach our nation for Jesus. It has a firm death grip on the throats of too many of our churches and is squeezing the very life out of them. We've got to be free of its influence once and for all, if we would see revival breakout in our homes, our churches, our cities, and in our nation!

Footnote: I heard that the old house that my friend loaned me burned down. I wonder if Cujo got out.

4

The 'Peter Pan' Skirt

What Do You Want To Be When You Grow Up?

E very time I hear someone say,
"Well, I'm just following my heart."
I want to scream at them,
"WHAT?!!! Are you NUTS?!!!"

"Listen to your teacher. Repeat after me:
I'll never grow up, never grow up, never grow up.
Not me!"   — Peter Pan [23]

S ome years ago I was pasturing a small mainline denominational church located in the rolling hills of east Tennessee. One night I was presiding over our regular monthly meeting of the Administrative Board. This gathering consisted of about ten elected officials who made up the governing body of our church. We met once a month to discuss and vote on current issues facing our congregation.

One of the topics of discussion this night was the new bulletin board. We had already bought it and it was a beauty. It was about three by four feet in diameter, with handy glass doors and illuminated interior. It was really very nice and everyone was pleased with it, but... there was a problem.

A Goliath had stepped into the meeting and challenged us all. I soon found myself facing a dilemma of gigantic proportion! If not handled with fervent prayer and painstaking delicacy, I knew that this crisis would have disastrous consequences. Here I'm talking a possible church split!

"Well, now that we have that beautiful new bulletin board where shall we put it?" I asked the board. "Any recommendations?"

"How about we hang it in the vestibule on the left wall," someone offered. "Across from the big picture of Jesus."

"Great idea!" I responded. "That way people can look at it coming in and out of the front door. Any other ideas?"

"Somebody's not gonna like that!" came a solemn remark from the other end of the table. It was ole rain-on-our-parade himself, Bro. Eeyore.

You know him don't you? You should! Every church has at least one Brother or a Sister Eeyore. Why, you might even be one yourself! It's not difficult to recognize them. Eeyore's, like Pooh Bear's little donkey friend, possess the unique gift of being able to point out the dark side of everything. And if they can't find one, they will create one. They are world renown for their uncanny ability to snatch defeat right out of the jaws of victory.

They also double as the church's dedicated volunteer firemen. They diligently watch for any sign of a Holy Spirit fire beginning to blaze up in the mist of the congregation. They then charge right in with their big wet blankets and beat it to death. It's their call in life to plant themselves in a local church and then stand in all-out opposition against anything that remotely resembles change. Bro. Eeyore is every pastor's worst nightmare!

"What do you mean, Bro. Eeyore?" I asked. "Well... that's where the attendance board has been hanging for the last sixty-two thousand, four hundred and fifteen years, six months, three days, eight hours and seventeen minutes, and if we move it... someone's going to get their *feelings* hurt."

My blood pressure began to rise and I felt my scalp tingle. I was Mount St. Helen with a giant cork stuck in it. "SOMEBODY'S GOING TO GET THEIR *FEELINGS* HURT IF WE MOVE THE ATTENDANCE BOARD!" I screamed *inside*. I was completely flabbergasted! Of all the asinine statements for someone to make, that one took the cake! I don't mean to imply that I'm a hothead who explodes at the least provocation, but this was just one of a long list of molehills turned into mountains from him since my pastorate there.

I wanted to blow my cork and scream at the top of my lungs, "WHAT ABOUT *GOD'S* FEELINGS?!" but I didn't. God's grace kicked in. I managed to maintain my cool through the remainder of the meeting and *didn't cuss even once!* We somehow settled the monumental task of deciding where to put the new bulletin board, took care of some other business, and then we adjourned.

After the meeting was thankfully over, I continued to bite my tongue long enough to shake hands with everyone and even managed a forced smile while shaking Bro. Eeyore's hand. (I'm such a hypocrite!) I managed a beaming, "See ya Sunday morning!" I then hopped into my V.W. Rabbit and fired up the engine. My windshield was beginning to fog from the steam rising up from my scalp. I hurried home as rapidly as I could, grumbling all the way. I climbed out of my car, stormed through the front door of my apartment and drop kicked the Pekingese over the rubber plant in my living room.

A religious man-centered attitude will oppose change at any cost. I repeat, at any cost! I've seen enough go-nowhere, do-nothing churches that are filled with not only gloomy ol' Eeyore's, but also with Peter Pans who *don't wanna grow up!* Their idea of progress is buying new cushions for the pews, new choir robes, or putting a fresh coat of paint on the building. There's never any real change and, therefore, no real growth. And that's just the way they like it.

*Instead, speaking the truth in love, we will in all things **grow up into him** who is the Head, that is, Christ.*
(Ephesians 4:15)

Growth = Change

We're going to discuss the necessity of personal change in chapter eight, but first I feel we need to lay some important groundwork before continuing.

As stated earlier, natural law dictates that when a thing stops growing it starts dying. Now, let's take this a step further. Growth *always* equals change. But on the other hand, change does not necessarily equal growth. Change must be in a *vertical* direction in order for that to happen.

When speaking of vertical change I'm referring to one's relationship with God and the impact it has on one's lifestyle. Vertical growth takes place *only* when one seeks God and finds one's relationship with him deepening. The resulting affect is a horizontal change in the way that we view our circumstances and our relationships with others. Being with God always results in some degree of change taking place—first vertically then ultimately horizontally. Motion in only a horizontal direction may bring about change in one's circumstance, surroundings or interpersonal relationships, but spiritual growth can be virtually nonexistent.

A person grows proportionately to how much they are willing to allow God to introduce change into their lives. I look back over the years and I see a lot of change. I don't look the way I did twenty-five years ago. I don't think the way I did, and I certainly don't do many of the things I did. Nor is my belief system the same as it was when I was twenty-one years old and embarking on this journey called life.

I find that the more I seek God and spend time in his presence, the more of a transformation I experience. If I look back on my life and I see no significant change, then I have a real problem. *Because if I am not changing, chances are I am not spending enough quality time with the LORD, through prayer and Bible study, and am therefore not growing. Then if I am not growing, I am dying!*

A True Vertical Experience or Mere Emotions?

Many of us confuse a mere emotional release with a vertical experience. I've seen it happen over and over again. It's a phenomenon that occurs quite often among us Christians who are more emotionally expressive in our worship—believers such as Pentecostals, Charismatics, and Baptists to mention a few. It's to misinterpret what is solely an emotional rush as an experience with God.

For example; many believers are misled into thinking that they have gotten a *touch* from God purely on the basis of some euphoric reaction to a few minutes of praise and worship music. They assume that they had a real vertical experience simply because they became emotional. To them what they *feel* gauges the depth of their spiritual experience. *Could it be, however, that they have not gotten in touch with God, but rather, have gotten in touch with their emotions?* The true test of a vertical experience is manifested in a horizontal chance.

> *"Not everyone who says to me, 'Lord, Lord,' will enter the kingdom of heaven, but only he who does the will of my Father who is in heaven."*
> — Jesus (Matthew 7:21)

Sadly, many assume that they have had a true salvation experience because of an emotional display at an altar. Still others mistake a wave of remorse and a few shed tears over some damaging behavioral pattern as repentance. An emotional outburst is often a part of the repentance process. However, like every true vertical experience it goes way beyond what one feels. So many have a death grip on that wrong skirt and are tangled in a web of deception because they allow their feelings to guide them rather than the Word of God.

The Blind Guide

*The heart is deceitful above all things and
beyond cure. Who can understand it?*
(Jeremiah 17:9)

" If a blind man leads a blind man, both will fall into a pit."
— Jesus (Matthew 15:14b)

It was June 1968. The place was Fort Campbell, Kentucky. Yours-truly was in Army basic infantry training. One day we marched all day and only took a break to do some training exercises. The D. I. (Drill Instructor), SSgt. Charles Smith, told us we were going to march over to the firing range for some nighttime target practice. So, we grabbed our backpacks, which by then weighed about 1000 Pounds, and our M-16 rifles. Then, SSgt. Smith marched us into the darkness. Now, when I say darkness; I don't mean a little stroll in the moonlight. There was no moon that night. We were deep in the Kentucky woods, shrouded by darkness as black as the Devil's heart.

To make matters worse, in order to get to the target range, we had to go down a precarious tank trail filled with one to two foot deep ruts caused by those huge metal monsters. SSgt. Smith shouted back at the platoon, "Round step... hooaahhh!!!" which is Drill Sergeant talk for, "You don't have to march in step. Just walk casually and stay in line. Now,... do it!" We tried our best to follow him but it was so dark we couldn't even see the person marching in front of us.

Then the unthinkable happened; SSgt. Smith got lost. There in the inking darkness he lost his way and of course we were lost right along with him. Undaunted, he continued leading us, first in one direction than another, hoping to find the tank trail somewhere. It soon became evident to all of us that we were being led by someone as blinded by the darkness as we were.

We walked along desperately trying to see. Occasionally one of us would trip and fall causing those behind to fall over him. I couldn't see what was happening but I could hear it. There were the sounds of men grunting and cursing as they stumbled over each other, crashing to the ground. Their helmets were rolling away and right in the path of their fellow troopers causing them to lose their footing and fall. We couldn't help laughing at what we heard. It was all very funny until it happened to one of us. Finally, after about 45 minutes of stumbling in the darkness, SSgt. Smith found the trail and we we're back on course.

Holding on to the wrong skirt can be like following a blind guide. We become lost in deep darkness when we follow something, or someone, other than the Holy Spirit. The same holds true when we latch onto some system of belief that we think came from the Holy Spirit.

We humans are complex emotional beings. Life studies have been made and Doctorates have been issued proclaiming certain individuals to be experts in the field of psychology. However, we may increase our knowledge of the human psyche but understanding it can be another thing. The word "heart' in the original Hebrew speaks of "the heart; also used (figuratively) very widely for the feelings, the will and even the intellect; likewise for the centre of anything"[24] God's word clearly states, *"Who can understand it?"* I believe that's what the Holy Spirit wants us to see in Jeremiah 17:9. The heart—the seat of emotions and the will—is the most deceitful thing in existence.

Every time I hear someone say, "Well, I'm just following my heart." I want to scream at them, "WHAT?!!! Are you NUTS?!!!" We must be very careful when it comes to following our feelings. They fluctuate according to the mood swings of a person. Follow-ing your heart can be a classic case of the blind leading the blind. You'll soon find yourself looking up from the bottom of a pit.

> *At this point Festus interrupted Paul's defense.*
> *"You are out of your mind, Paul!" he shouted.*
> *"Your great learning is driving you insane."*
> (Acts 26:24)

You maybe thinking by now that ol' Rod's elevator doesn't go all the way to the top, that he has a few cobwebs in the windmills of his mind. Perhaps the light in his attic has begun to flicker. Well, there maybe some truth in that, depending on who you talk to. However, please permit me to explain to any Festus' who are reading this.

I'm not saying that Christians should be devoid of emotions. Absolutely not! We already have too many *deadpans* occupying our pews who look like someone just ran over their dog. You couldn't move them with a stick of dynamite. Their favorite hymn is "Just like a tree that's planted by the waters, *I shall not be moved.*"[25]

No, that's not what I'm saying at all. Love is perhaps the most powerful emotion there is and when I'm in the presence of God... I *feel* love. In fact, I've experience a kaleidoscope of sensations that are often overwhelming when I've been in God's presence and sensed his Spirit. So emotions are definitely a part, but only a part, of experiencing God. It is not the whole.

"But, Rod," you may be thinking. "I've worshiped God and it felt as if I was floating! I mean, as high as a kite! Why, I've danced before the Lord and have even *fallen out* when the preacher laid hands on me. I remember a few times that I got so caught up in the Spirit that I just wept for hours. It felt wonderful!"

Then others may say, "Why, I've been to services where they shouted the house down! People were jumping over pews and prophesying to beat the band! Boy, what a time we had! That's got to be God! Now, *that's* a vertical experience if there ever was one, Rod, and don't you say it wasn't. *You heathen!*"

Distinguishing the truth from the False —The Acid Test

You may be shocked to hear me say that I agree with you. All of the above can be valid vertical experiences if... I repeat, *if* you walk away from such an experience having been impacted in some life-changing way. My friend, since the dawn of time *every encounter that man has had with Holy God has resulted in some form of radical change in their lives.* They underwent all sorts of transformation from life changes to name changes. They became different people then they were before their encounter with Holy God.

The scripture says that our God is a consuming fire[26]. Therefore, a true vertical experience will result in repentance and purging. Only then does righteous change takes place, first vertically and then horizontally. *If there is no change to your character resulting from your "experience with God", then you did not get in touch with God. You got in touch with your emotions.*

Repentance — One of the most misunderstood Doctrines of the Church

> *"First to those in Damascus, then to those in Jerusalem and in all Judea, and to the Gentiles also, I preached that they should repent and turn to God and prove their repentance by their deeds."* — Paul
> (Acts 26:20)

Before continuing it is important to understand the meaning of true biblical repentance; especially when you consider what is a true vertical experience. What is repentance? First, let's look at what it's not. Repentance is not simple remorse over one's sins. Prisons are full of remorseful people. Many just lament over getting caught while others are truly sorry for what they did. Strong's says that the Greek word for *repentance* means to "change one's mind, i.e. to repent, to change one's mind for better, heartily to amend with abhorrence of one's past sins". [27]

For several years I was corresponding with the man who was once the infamous *Son of Sam* killer. David Berkowitz gave his life to the LORD many years ago. He no longer calls himself *The Son of Sam*. He is now *The Son of Hope*. David had a true vertical experience when he repented and surrendered his life to Jesus. He has therefore turned his incarceration into a ministry to both those inside prison and those outside. His life is a blessing to everyone he encounters.

In a letter David sent to New York Governor George E. Pataki he shows a true heart of repentance. He writes concerning his June 2002 parole hearing:

"I am haunted by my actions and I would do anything to undo this tragedy. I know that I have failed and disappointed my loving family, and I disgraced myself for the rest of my life. However today, because of Jesus Christ and my faith in Him, I am trying my best to make amends to society in any way that I can. And I am thankful for whatever opportunities which come my way to do this …

"In all honesty, I believe that I deserve to be in prison for the rest of my life. I have, with God's help, long ago come to terms with my situation and I have accepted my punishment. God has given me peace about this. My faith has helped to put the past behind me and to always pray for those whom I have hurt, and those who are still grieving till this very day.

"Sir, it is so tragic and regrettable that the families of my victims have to go through more suffering. Right now they're filled with anger, anxiety and pain because they think I am trying hard to get out of prison. But this is simply not true.   Governor Pataki, these people have nothing to worry about. For if and when I go to this hearing, it will only be to show respect to the parole board, to apologize and take responsibility for my criminal actions, and to basically tell them what I am now telling you – that I do not deserve parole. (underscore David's)

"Thank you, your honor, for taking the time to read my letter. I hope it has brought some clarity to this matter. I pray dearly that these families will be able to have some peace and closure very soon."[28]

Now, that's what I call proof of a true vertical experience. Repentance, a change of mind/attitude and the desire to change one's life, is where the rubber meets the road. Over the years in my correspondence with David, he has clearly shown a true heart of repentance. The gentleness and the sweetness of his spirit are interwoven into every line that he writes and I'm proud to call David my friend.

"Prove by the way you live that you have really turned from your sins and turned to God. " — John the Baptizer
(Matthew 3:8) [29]

Transformation

You say that you've been in the presence of the Lord today? Is that right? May I ask you something? Have you gone through a change of mind and heart? Or do you still resist transformation? Do you still refuse to repent of old behavioral habits that cause you to treat others with unkindness? Do you still walk in rebellion to clear revelation from God's word for your life?

Husbands, do you still refuse to love and honor your wife? Do you refuse to treat her with dignity and kindness? How about you wives? Do you still refuse to show respect to your husband and honor him in the way that God's Word commands?

My friend, do you still cheat on your taxes? Do you treat your brother unjustly? Do you refuse to forgive others? Do you pass judgment on those who disagree with you? If so, then keep your great church services and all your glory-hallelujah experiences to yourself, because they don't amount to a bag of hair in light of a true encounter with the life-changing God.

> In the Presence of your glory,
> all my crowns lie in the dust.
> You are righteous in your judgments,
> Lord, you are faithful, true, and just.
> And I cry holy, holy, holy God,
> how awesome is your name,
> Holy, holy, holy God,
> how majestic is your name,
> And I am changed in the Presence of a Holy God[30]

Spiritual Junkies

> *"You hypocrites!*
> *Isaiah was right when he prophesied about you:*
> *'These people honor me with their lips,*
> *but their hearts are far from me.*
> *They worship me in vain;*
> *their teachings are but rules taught by men."*
> — Jesus (Matthew. 15:7-9)

"The greatest *Aman* you can give the word of God is obedience!"
— T.D. Jakes[31]

We love to sing the song, *We bring the sacrifice of
praise... into the house of the Lord!*[32] However, too many times
we forget that, *"To obey is better than sacrifice... "*[33] God is not
the least bit interested in our "lip" service. Moreover, God most
certainly doesn't offer the joy of his presence to a rebellious
people who seem bent on ignoring the dictates of his Word.
God doesn't offer a true personal experience with him to a self-
indulged generation, who does not seek God but rather seek ways
in which they may *work up* the Spirit in hopes of receiving some
sort of paranormal buzz.

We've become a bunch of spiritual junkies who have
overlooked God in our quest for an emotional fix. *To put it
bluntly, the Bride of Christ has shunned the intimacy of her loving
Husband and instead has engaged in spiritual masturbation.*

Perhaps my choice of words will offend the sensibilities
of some. Some may consider me rude, crude, or even downright
vulgar. But quite frankly, I was much more concerned that I
might offend my God than I was about offending someone's
sensitivities. Please, don't dismiss this as someone trying to be
clever or controversial. I prayerfully spent a lot of time writing
and rewriting that last paragraph. I sought to express myself in
a way that would leave a lasting impression on the reader of just
how terribly we have offended our wonderful Lord!

A Discernment Deficiency

The Church needs to be made painfully aware of our
disgraceful conduct. I felt genuinely impressed by the Holy Spirit

with this image. It was one so graphic, so profound that it first drove *me* to repentance. It is such a vivid picture of what is a clearly shameful behavior.

So, if you are offended by my choice of words more than you are ashamed by our disgraceful treatment of our Lord, then I fear that you have a serious discernment deficiency! You need to come out of the darkness, my friend. I pray that the eyes of your understanding may be opened before it's too late and you never get a chance to enjoy the intimacy of our loving Lord.

Making Adjustments

Change is commonplace for the true God-seeker. God-seekers are constantly undergoing a metamorphosis of mind and spirit. They experience true transformation, because they yield themselves to the lordship of Christ. They make the necessary adjustments no matter what the cost. It may be frightening and uncomfortable at times, but the rewards are beyond compare.

However, while many are pressing on and seeking God, others are not. Instead, the non-seeker chooses the mundane, the nominal, *the same-ol' same-ol'*. They cling tightly to that *Peter Pan skirt* and refuse to grow up. Those who do decide to go on, however, will experience a daily change *and* a daily growth. Most importantly, they will reap the awesome joy of having an intimate relationship with God! (We'll take a closer look at what it means to truly know God in chapter nine.)

Paul, the Yuppie — An Example of Vertical Change

Change can be frightening to us mortals! It is nonetheless essential if we would grow up in Christ. Don't kid yourself. If we desire to go on with God personal change will take place in our lives, and change is often no picnic. It can be an overwhelming struggle to take your human nature to task. However, it must be done. Be aware that true vertical experiences bring about radical change that is frequently confusing and painful.

God is more interested in us becoming more
like Christ than he is in comfort.

There are many examples in the Bible that describe the impact a serious encounter with God can have on someone. For example, it must have been very alarming to a man named Saul to have a vertical experience completely overturn his horizontal world. Nothing in his life was quite the same after that aborted mission to Damascus.

Before Saul became Paul, he was experiencing rapid horizontal change in his life. He was an up and coming young man who was climbing the political and religious ladder. He was self-confident, very aggressive and was admired and respected by his peers.

Young Saul was a classic example of a first century Yuppie. He began his life as an unknown Jew from Tarsus. He acquired the finest education available and eventually became a member of the highest Jewish court in the land—the Sanhedrin; a position that brought him much wealth and honor. This was quite an accomplishment wouldn't you say? He was eventually elevated to a position of such trust that he was chosen to spearhead the vicious campaign to stomp out the early church. Saul was decidedly one of the movers and shakers of his day. His world saw considerable change transpire. No doubt he and his piers understood it to be dramatic growth, but was it?

Conforming to a *What* Rather Than a Spiritual *Who*

I repeat, change does not always constitute spiritual growth. That is if the change takes place only on a horizontal plane. Saul was like many of today's church members. He was locked into a religious worldview that became the pattern by which he fashioned his life. The result being that he let his religion come between him and God! In other words, his religious zeal blocked any vertical growth.

"How can this be?" you may ask. Saul spent a major portion of his life studying the law until he knew it like he knew the back of his hand. Saul knew the law; he just didn't know the Law Giver. Saul was like so many contemporary church members. *He dedicated his life to becoming conformed to his religious ideology rather than to God's character.* And therein lies the rub.

This attitude so reflects that of the church in America. We've gotten our little religious ducks all in a row. We wave our denominational banners in each other's faces and shout at others in the body of Christ, "Weeearrree rii-ght! Yourrr-rr raaw-ing! Neh, neh, neh, neh-neh... neh!"

Each sect thinks that they have exclusive possession of the truth. The problem one faces when adopting such an elitist attitude is that it *always* interferes with one's relationship with God. It always stifles change and, therefore, impedes growth. This happens because *it demands conformity — not to the image of God's son but, rather, to the guidelines of their particular belief system.*

An Attitude Test

How about your church? Is it a progressive, constantly changing, constantly growing, vibrant body that displays God's love to others? Or is it an unmoving, unchanging, uncaring, non-growing, dead congregation? Does this latter description portray your church?

"Oh no! Not *our* church!" you may protest. "Why... we're a Bible believing church—a Christ-centered church! We're not like those *other* churches. Us... afraid of change? We always encourage our members to strive to become conformed to the character of God. Plus, we're a progressive church as well. Why, we reach out to everyone. Yes sir-ree! That's *our* church!" I sincerely hope so.

May I offer a little questionnaire designed to confirm whether or not your church is as progressive, loving, and accepting as you believe it to be? This simple questionnaire will remove all doubts as to whether or not you belong to a church that truly reflects the character of Christ. Please check the appropriate response: (Pray before answering and *please, be honest.)*

"Then you will know the truth, and the truth will set you free."
— Jesus (John 8:32)

1) Other races are warmly welcomed.
ALWAYS___SOMETIMES___NEVER___

2) Our communion service is open to people of other denominations.
ALWAYS___SOMETIMES___NEVER___

3) We recognize another believer's baptism even if it wasn't administered by our church or denomination.
ALWAYS___SOMETIMES___NEVER___

4) We gladly offer our pulpit to other anointed preachers who are not a part of our church, denomination or movement.
ALWAYS___SOMETIMES___NEVER___

5) People who have experienced divorce are used in leadership capacities.
ALWAYS___SOMETIMES___NEVER___

6) Interracial couples are warmly welcomed.
ALWAYS___SOMETIMES___NEVER___

7) Unwed mothers and their children are welcomed.
ALWAYS___SOMETIMES___NEVER___

8) Junkies, derelicts, and alcoholics are routinely found in our congregation.
ALWAYS___SOMETIMES___NEVER___

9) We welcome open discussion concerning different scriptural viewpoints and even use teaching materials from outside of our church or denomination.
ALWAYS___ SOMETIMES___NEVER___

10) Our church is actively involved in training soul winners and there are daily reports of people coming to Jesus throughout the week.
ALWAYS___ SOMETIMES___NEVER___

Well, how did you do? I hope you could honestly answer, ALWAYS on all ten questions. But if you could not, perhaps you should arrange a meeting with your church's leadership to discuss ways of correcting the direction that your congregation is heading. If such a meeting results in a negative response to your inquiry, or worst yet indifference, then I strongly suggest that you shake the dust off of your feet[34] and get yourself and your family out of that church.

Prayerfully look for a church that is constantly stretching and changing, for that is a church that is horizontally driven as it's vertically directed. It's a church that's truly seeking God. Look for one that readily embraces everyone in the community. Find a body of believers who rejects sin but loves and reaches out to the sinner. Seek a church that desires truth at any cost and wants to rid themselves of the religious rats that plague their individual lives. Don't give up until you've found it. For when you've found a church like that, you've found a rare treasure.

5

THE 'PET DOCTRINE' SKIRT

How Much Is That Doctrine
In The Window?

W e must come together
on that one common ground that binds us all
—the love we have for Jesus and each other.

"I appeal to you, brothers, in the name of our Lord Jesus Christ, that all of you agree with one another so that there may be no divisions among you and that you may be perfectly united in mind and thought...."
— The Apostle Paul (1 Corinthians 1:10-11)

I f there's anything that we Christians have it's doctrines. We've got them running out of our ears. Now, there's obviously nothing wrong with doctrines. It's very important to not only know *what* you believe, but *why* you believe. Yes doctrines are good as long as we don't let them divide us.

We followers of Christ have doctrines on every conceivable subject. Unfortunately, we have used our doctrines like so many bricks to build walls to separate us from those Christians with whom we disagree. Like I said; there's nothing wrong with having doctrines. Just don't let them come between you and the church down the street.

Yes, we do have a wide range of doctrines. We've got doctrines about salvation. Is it salvation by faith alone, or do you have to mix a little works in with it? And if so, how much do you add? What's too much? What's too little? When does grace give way to personal performance? *Inquiring minds want to know.*

When we become Christians how well does it stick? Is it "Once saved always saved?" Or is it a "Pray that I'll make it through!" salvation? Maybe everything is already mapped out for us and we really don't have much of a choice in the matter. You're already predestined to go to Heaven or Hell.

Then we've got doctrines about baptism. Do you dunk them? Do you dip them? Do you sprinkle or pour water on them? And if you dunk them, how far under do you go? Do you sort of give them a quick dip like you would a donut, or do you hold them under, like Christian comedian Mike Warnke said, "Until they really repent?!"

If you sprinkle or pour, how much water do you use? How

wet do you get them? Where is the cutting off place? How do you know when you've used just the right amount of water? How much does it take? Does it take a bucket full, a glass full, or is it like the old Bril Cream commercial for hair styling gel, "A little dab a do yah."

Once you've ascertained the proper method of baptizing someone and have figured out the correct amount of water, you must then decide who is allowed to do it. Should only the pastor of a church be allowed to baptize, or can a pastor who is between churches do it as well? How about a deacon or an elder? Perhaps an evangelist is allowed to do it... then again, maybe not.

Here's a biggie—the second coming of Christ! Boy do we fight over that one! Are you pre-millennial? And if so, are you historical or dispensational? Perhaps you are post-millennial, mid-millennial or a-millennial. It could be that you are pan-millennial; which is the belief that it's all going to pan out in the end the way God wants it to. So why fuss over it?

The body is a unit, though it is made up of many parts;
*and though all its parts are many, **they form one body.***
So it is with Christ. For we were all baptized
by one Spirit into one body.
(1 Corinthians 12:12-13)

We split hairs over everything from which translation of the Bible we read to whether or not to use real wine for communion service. I agree that variety is the spice of life. God is a god of infinite variety. Just look at nature. The works of his hands are a continual testimony to this. However, it takes everything on this planet, no matter how vastly different, to make our ecosystem.

So it is with the Church. *It takes all of us along with our different perspectives to make up the Church as a whole. We therefore desperately need each other, no matter our secondary differences.* We must come together on that one common ground that binds us all—the love we have for Jesus and each other.

A Lesson from an Elephant

Three blind men, who had been friends for many years, decided to take a trip to a petting zoo. They had never gone before, so they were very excited. Being blind from birth, they had only heard about many of these beautiful, exotic, animals, but had never *touched* them or experienced firsthand what they were. Upon arrival, they immediately found a tour guide who took them directly to the place where the animals were located.

Their hearts were filled with awe as they slowly went from animal to animal, savoring each touch, each stroke of warm silken fur along with the hodgepodge of different smells and sounds. Eventually, they arrived at a lot where an animal resided that was completely unfamiliar to them. They made their way into the enclosed area and carefully approached. They listened but heard only the sounds of heavy breathing accompanied by an occasional snorting noise.

They were carefully drawing closer when suddenly a trumpet blasted and a gust of warm, damp, air struck them in the face sending their hats soaring through the air! The very ground quaked beneath their feet as this massive beast shifted his weight! The men bolted and started in three directions. As they were

fleeing, arms began to gently encircle them and a voice softly
saying, "It's O.K... It's O.K. There's nothing to fear. He won't
hurt you... I promise!"

As their shaken nerves began to settle, they recognized
the voice of their guide. "You guys all right?" "Yes. I... ah think
so." one of them said as he took a deep breath. "What was that?!"
"Why... that's an elephant!" replied the puzzled guide. 'Haven't
you ever seen... ah, I mean." "No we haven't." responded another.
"Is it safe to touch him?" "Oh yes!" the tour guide beamed back.
"Help yourself!" And with that, he gathered up their hats and then
escorted them to a position within reach of this strange creature.

Armed with the calm, reassuring, voice of their tour guide
they proceeded to reach out, touch, and discover for themselves
just what an elephant is like. One felt of the animal's short slender
tail. "Why, an elephant is like a snake!" he exclaimed. "No!" said
the one standing at the other end. "An elephant is like a tree!"
He smiled triumphantly as he continued stroking the animal's
long leathery trunk. "No... wrong again!" retorted the one in the
middle, as he rubbed the elephant's side. "You're both *waaaay*
off base. It's obvious that an elephant is like a wall." He then
chuckled scornfully at their ridiculous solutions to an obviously
simple riddle. "How could you *both* be so mistaken?!" he asked.
"What?!" they both answered in unison. "*You're* the one that's
off base! It's like a tree!" the one at the head shouted. "Did you
guys check in your brains at the gate or something?!" laughed the
one standing at the end. "It's like a snake! I mean, how *stupid* can
anyone be?!"

"Who you calling stupid?!! STUPID!" The middleman
chimed in. "Yeah!" the other echoed. "*You're* the one who's

stupid! Anyone who says an elephant is like a snake is off the… *stupid rector scale!"* He then broke free of the others and stormed out the gate, knocking down a little old lady who was feeding popcorn to a monkey. "Why, I never," she exclaimed, as the squealing monkey grabbed her popcorn bag and scurried up a nearby tree.

The other two followed suit, exiting the petting zoo with white canes flailing about and shouting angrily at one another. The tour guide watched in amazement as the crowd quickly divided, making a path for three crazy men, waving canes and yelling at the top of their lungs. The three of them boarded separate buses, departed and never spoke to one another again. They allowed their different perspectives to destroy the friendship that they had treasured for so long.

What these men failed to realize was that they were all correct! Yet at the same time they were all wrong in their assessment that their opinion was the only valid response to the question, "What is an elephant like?" The different parts of an elephant do resemble a snake, a wall, and a tree. Each perspective needed to be heard in order to get a true picture.

Fitting the Pieces Together

My long time buddy, Stan Beaver, gave me an excellent illustration that deserves passing on. We were hanging out one evening after church for some food and fellowship. I was airing my concern about division in the Church when Stan interrupted. "Rod," he said over a partially devoured Whopper and large order of fries, "Each of 'em (mainline denominations) has a piece of the puzzle. The Baptists have a piece. The Pentecostals have a piece.

The Methodists have one, the Charismatics, Nazarenes, all of 'em. They've all got a piece!"

He paused while chewing on a handful of fries and then leaned over on his elbows. He drew on his straw and swallowed a massive amount of Dr. Pepper, looked back up and squinted his eyes. "The problem is... that it takes *all* the pieces of the puzzle to make the picture." He then added with an explosion of passion, "And we can't get along with each other long enough to see *what* the picture is!!"

His point was well taken. As long as God's people major on the minors, there's going to be continued strife and division. If we split hairs with our brothers and sisters over our differences and refuse to receive from their ministries, purely on the basis of secondary theological differences, we will never have the whole picture.

> *The Christ has been divided into various parts,*
> *with the present result that He lies there broken up*
> *into fragments which are distributed among you.*
> (1 Corinthians 1:13)[35]

What is the whole picture? Why, it's Jesus of course! How is the church going to impact this nation unless we present a clear and complete picture of Jesus in all his fullness? *If we would see this country healed and renewed to greatness, we must cast our petty differences aside and begin to walk together.* For only then can we learn from one another and thus put the fragments together. Then we will be able to present a true representation of Jesus to a world that is desperate to know if he's real and if he can help them.

Justifying Division

Do two walk together unless they have agreed to do so?
(Amos 3:3)

The American church is going to have to make a decision; no, a commitment to sit aside our secondary doctrinal differences, meet on common ground, and start walking together. Sadly, many have taken the King James Version of Amos 3:3, "Can two walk together, except they be agreed?" and have used it as some shallow justification for their rejection of other churches or denominations. They refuse to network with the rest of the Body of Christ in reaching our communities. Then they dismiss their pathetic behavior with the worn out cliché, "We're not in agreement."

As incredulous as it sounds, many have built an entire theological base that promotes strife and division *solely* on the basis of Elizabethan vernacular! The word "agreed" in the King James Bible text comes from the Hebrew word which means to make an appointment to meet with someone.[36] It has absolutely nothing to do with agreeing philosophically or theologically with someone.

*"My prayer is not for them alone. I pray also for those who will believe in me through their [the apostle's] message, that all of them may be one, Father, just as you are in me and I am in you. May they also be in us so that the world may believe that you have sent me. I have given them the glory that you gave me, that they may be one as we are one: I in them and you in me. **May they be brought to complete unity to let the world know that you sent me and have loved them even as you have loved me.**" — Jesus (John 17:20-23)*

We must lay aside petty differences, obey God's Word, and extend hands of fellowship to others in the Church. We must *agree* to walk together. I'm not saying that we should all move into the same building; that would be too much to ask of most Christians. But rather, it is time that we quit splitting hairs by majoring on the minors and once for all become united in mission and purpose.

Common Ground

I appeal to you, brothers, in the name of our Lord Jesus Christ, that all of you agree with one another so that there may be no divisions among you and that you may be perfectly united in mind and thought.
(1 Corinthians 1:10)

The Greek word for *agree* in this passage is *lego*. The KJV renders it, *"speak the same things."* Vine's says, *"lego* refers especially to the substance of what is said."[37] He further explains that this is as opposed to the actual words being spoken." Paul is not necessarily demanding that we all see eye to eye on every issue. However, he is stating emphatically that we believers are to make the *message* that we preach carry the same theme. What is that theme? Let's go back to the Apostle Paul for the answer.

When I came to you, brothers, I did not come with eloquence or superior wisdom as I proclaimed to you the testimony about God. For I resolved to know nothing while I was with you except Jesus Christ and him crucified.
(1 Corinthians 2:1-2)

> *A cord of three strands is not quickly broken.*
> (Ecclesiastes 4:12)

Together we must use every means at our disposal to preach *Jesus Christ and him crucified.* I believe this is what is meant when we speak of having the *power of agreement. There is power when the Church speaks with one voice, one massage.* In Church unity there is an authority that sends chills up Satan back. As the binding of cords produces a stronger rope, the binding together of believers in love, purpose, and the mutual goal of reaching the lost will endure the Body of Believers with unbeatable power!

Sadly, the contemporary Church offers little power, because we refuse to walk together, and from division springs weakness. This is partly what Jesus meant when he said, "Every kingdom divided against itself will be ruined, and every city or household divided against itself will not stand."[38] A divided church is a weak church. It, therefore, takes very little to topple it.

Sending an S.O.S. to a Watching World

> "If not for Christians, I'd be a Christian."
> "I like your Christ; I do not like your Christians.
> Your Christians are so unlike your Christ."
> These quotes attributed to Mohandas Gandhi[39]

> "It's going to take a different kind of church
> than we have now to impress the world."
> — Dr. Roy Cantrell[40]

It really doesn't matter whether you like it or not; we *are* being carefully scrutinized. Don't make the mistake of thinking that people are dim-witted just because they haven't surrendered to Jesus. Moreover, neither are they blind or deaf. They see and hear what goes on in this *family feud* that we affectionately call "The Church."

A man had been stranded alone on a small island for 25 years. One day a passing ship saw a huge fire on the beach and came to his rescue. After getting him on board the ship, the captain asked him some questions about what it was like being marooned all that time.

> "Sir", the captain said. "When we arrived on the beach I noticed that you had three grass cabins standing side by side. You were alone weren't you?"
> "Yes I was, Captain." he responded
> "Then, why were there three huts when you were there all by yourself?"
> "Well," the man answered. "The cabin on the far right is where I live and the cabin in the middle is where I go to church."
> Puzzled, the captain inquired further, "What about the cabin on the far left? What's it for?"
> A smirk spread across the man's darkly tanned face and he said, "Oh… that's where I *used* to go to church."

I was attempting to witness to a man I worked with some years ago who was very hardened to the gospel. As time progressed, he became increasingly hostile toward me. Then one day, he exploded at me with words full of hurt and anger. "All you Christians are a bunch of people who fuss and fight all the time!

Everyone thinks they're right and everyone else is wrong! You're just a bunch of hypocrites who fuss and fight all the time! Just answer me one question... *just one!"* He demanded, his face was turning crimson, "Why would *I* want to be apart of anything like that?!"

He finished his spiel and stood there defiantly awaiting an answer. But I had none to give. That is, I had none to offer that would placate the bitter sense of disgust and disappointment he felt.

Oh, I could have offered a few canned responses but he deserved better. *The world deserves better than what the Church all too often offers.* I stood there in stunned silence unable, or perhaps too embarrassed to answer. He had shamed me into silence. To a great extent what he had said was true.

Our divisiveness speaks volumes to those around us. It tells a watching world that protecting our peculiar piece of the puzzle is clearly more important to us than they are. Our *majoring on the minors* says that we have nothing genuine to offer. We offer nothing unique because what we present is not much different than that which they already have. *It's just S.O.S.— the Same Old Stuff they get from the world around them—dissension, feuding, duplicity, and mistrust.*

Famous Saints Speak Out
• Martin Luther
"I ask that men make no reference to my name, and call themselves not Lutherans, but Christians. What is Luther? My doctrine, I am sure, is not mine, nor have I been crucified for any one. St. Paul, in I Cor. iii, would not allow Christians to call

themselves Pauline or Petrine, but Christian. How then should I, poor, foul carcass that I am, come to have men give to the children of Christ a name derived from my worthless name? No, no, my dear friends; let us abolish all party names, and call ourselves Christians after Him Whose doctrine we have." – (Hugh Thomson Kerr, *A Compend of Luther's Theology*, Philadelphia: The Westminster Press, 1943, p. 135. Also cited by Lewis W. Spitz, Ph. D., *Our Church and Others*, Saint Louis, MO: Concordia Publishing House, 1969, pp. 23-24.)

- John Wesley

"Would to God that all party names, and unscriptural phrases and forms which have divided the Christian world, were forgot and that the very name [Methodist-SGD] might never be mentioned more, but be buried in eternal oblivion." – (John Wesley, *Universal Knowledge, A Dictionary and Encyclopedia of Arts, Science, History, Biography, Law, Literature, Religions, Nations, Races, Customs, and Institutions, Vol. 9*, Edward A. Pace, Editor, New York: Universal Knowledge Foundation, 1927, p. 540)

- Charles Spurgeon

"I say of the Baptist name, let it perish, but let Christ's name last forever. I look forward with pleasure to the day when there will not be a Baptist living! I hope that the Baptist name will soon perish, but let Christ's name last forever." -- (*Spurgeon Memorial Library, Vol. I*, n.d., p. 168.)

- George Washington

"Of all the animosities which have existed among mankind, those which are caused by difference of sentiments in religion appear to be the most inveterate and distressing, and ought most to be deprecated. I was in hopes that the enlightened and liberal policy, which has marked the present age, would at least have reconciled

Christians of every denomination so far that we should never again see the religious disputes carried to such a pitch as to endanger the peace of society." -- [George Washington, letter to Edward Newenham, October 20, 1792; from George Seldes, ed., *The Great Quotations*, Secaucus, New Jersey: Citadel Press, 1983, p. 726]

- The Apostle Paul

"My brothers, some from Chloe's household have informed me that there are quarrels among you. What I mean is this: One of you says, "I follow Paul"; another, "I follow Apollos"; another, "I follow Cephas"; still another, "I follow Christ." Is Christ divided? Was Paul crucified for you? ere you baptized into the name of Paul?"   (1 Corinthians 1:11-13)

We cannot change our cities, much less the world, unless we first dismiss these destructive, divisive, attitudes and change the way we behave toward our fellow believers. We *must* lay aside petty differences, put an end to denominational flag waving, and start walking together in love. We must work together toward a common goal—reaching our cities with the Gospel. Then, and *only* then, will the world see the genuine article—the whole picture. Only then will God fill us with the power needed to bring revival to our city, our state, and yes, even our nation.

6

THE 'CONCRETE' SKIRT

The Danger Of Making Assumptions

It's not enough just to have an intellectual knowledge
of the truth; one must embrace it and hold on to it.

"But when He, the Spirit of truth, comes,
He will guide you into all truth.

— Jesus (John 16:13)

Y ou may find this hard to believe, but we so called *Spirit-filled Christians* are just as subject to religious deception as the rest of the church. In fact, we can also be just as vicious, as my old adversary Cujo, when our pet doctrines are challenged. We can be divisive, judgmental, and brazenly arrogant!

Many of us love to label ourselves as being "Full Gospel" and often deride other Christians who don't see things quite the way we do on the spiritual gifts[41] issue. What do we mean when we use that term anyway? Sadly, many have unknowingly used this term, "Full Gospel", erroneously. We Charismatic/Pentecostals have waved this idiom like a banner of pride and, in so by doing, have alienated the rest of The Church. We've even accused others of not preaching the *full,* or whole Gospel, simply because they do not advocate our doctrine. What a shame!

What does it mean to be filled with/by the Holy Spirit? Why all the controversy, anyway? *Could it be that we've become guilty of having the wrong emphasis?* Is it possible that we Charismatic/Pentecostals have become so obsessed with amplifying the *what,* that we have ignored the *why.* Why does the Holy Spirit fill believers in the first place? Let me elaborate by first sharing my own experience.

Becoming Supercharged!

I surrendered my life to Jesus just before my twelfth birthday, but my Christianity was fairly nominal until the summer before my sophomore year of High School. Something happened to me that could only be described as momentous. It was the beginning of a whole new era in my life that left me permanently transformed.

My parents, three brothers, and I were living in a little town nestled in the foothills of eastern Tennessee called Niota. It was a great place for a kid to grow up. Everybody knew each other. The streets were safe. Folks could leave their doors unlocked and their windows open at night. It was typical small town America and I loved it!

Although she was small, Niota boasted of having two factories that employed 70% of the town's residents. We had a barbershop that had two, count 'em, *two* chairs and a post office. We even had our own library. (I went there to check out a book once but somebody had already checked it out.)

That little town had two skating rinks, two old fashioned neighborhood grocery stores, a furniture store, a bank, a watch repairer, and a Chinese Theater. I have no idea what a Chinese Theater is actually. As far I know there were no Chinese actors or other kinds of entertainers there. The theater was actually the older and somewhat more dilapidated of the two skating rinks. On certain nights, it doubled as a movie theater. You had to bring throw pillows and sit, or recline, on the floor because there were no chairs. [Wormy Black, the town constable, would later shut it down because some of the patrons of the Chinese Theater were doing something other than watching the movie]

There were three churches within the township. The First Baptist Church, Niota Methodist, and the little congregation my dad pastored. East Niota Baptist Church had a group of warm supportive people, a renowned choir, and was home sweet home for the Davis' for better than seven years.

One fateful day the three churches put their heads and hearts together and prayerfully decided to have a citywide revival. The city park located in the heart of town was agreed upon as the best possible location. We then put up a large meeting tent and about 200 folding chairs. We printed some handouts and rented a battery operated briefcase size public address system.

I was especially thrilled over that little P.A. You see, I had just gotten my brand, spanking, new driver's license and my nervous dad reluctantly allowed me to drive around town with the P.A. strapped to the roof of the family car and make announcements about the revival. "Come to the city wide revival… in the park!" You could hear my youthful voice echoing up and down the alleyways and streets. Dogs barked at me and people stopped what they were doing and stared as we passed by.

My younger brother, Joe, came along with me and boy did we have a time! The two of us felt like big shots, driving here and there, taking turns on the microphone, giggling and poking fun at each other. These are some of my fondest memories, but the one memory that summer that left the most vivid impression on me is what happened to me midway through that two-week event.

One of my daily responsibilities, assigned to me by my dad, was to go down to the meeting site about an hour before the service to raise the sides of the tent. That way the fresh summer breeze would have time to air out the tent and cool it a bit before people started arriving.

God had been dealing intensely with me for days. Even though I knew I was a Christian, I didn't act very much like one. Often I viewed being a pastor's son as something of a stigma because I had to endure considerable teasing from my peers at school. Not only that, I was also under the constant scrutiny of the community where we lived.

So in order to prevent much of the embarrassment I felt at school, I became adept at keeping my *light* hidden from my friends through the week. Then on Sunday morning I would drag it out from underneath the bush where it was concealed, dust it off, and put it back on its lamp stand.

When Monday morning rolled around I would carefully take *this little light of mine* and cover it up again, placing it in my secret hiding place. There it would stay until the following Sunday. However, this cycle of intimidation and weakness that had me bound was soon to end forever!

One balmy summer evening I went down to the park to perform my daily ritual—*The Rising of the Tent Flaps*. However, this particular afternoon would be different from the others. This time I would deviate from my usual routine. This time I would wait a few minutes before raising the flaps. This time I would look around to see if anyone would notice a youthful figure silently vanishing behind the canvas walls of the tent. Yes, this time would be different. I was about to have an encounter with Holy God and my life would never be the same.

Quietly, I stepped into the tent's dimly lit interior. The burned smell of canvas baking in the summer sun greeted me. Its pungent aroma mingled with other more familiar summer scents, such as the smell of the grass and leaves. The hodgepodge of fragrances hung heavily in the air of that closed-in arena.

I made my way through the folding chairs and slowly, humbly, approached the altar. As I look back to that day it isn't difficult to imagine what it must have felt like to those high priests of old as one of them made his way past the crowds of worshipers and hopefuls who gathered around yet another tent all those years ago. The fear and awesome reverence he must have felt as he cautiously slipped through the veil and entered The Most Holy Place.

A similar reverential awe overwhelmed me as I, a lesser priest, entered yet another consecrated place and kneeled before Holy God. As I knelt there at the small wooden altar, I soon found myself weeping and calling out to him in my childish ignorance. For the first time I saw my reluctance to share my faith as it truly was—*cowardice*. I begged God to forgive me. I asked him to fill me with boldness to witness and with the power to do so.

He did just that. The presence of God was so strong and I realized that this was no chance meeting. This was an appointment that was set in eternity. Because of what was happing to me I would never be the same.

I made a fresh commitment to the Lordship of Jesus Christ that day and he filled me to capacity with his precious Holy Spirit. I didn't leap over any pews, speak in tongues, or prophecy. There were no rockets going off. As a matter of fact, there was no visual supernatural manifestation at all!

What did happen, however, was precisely what Jesus said would happen. "But you will receive *power* when the Holy Spirit comes on you; and you will be my witnesses."[42] The Greek construction of this verse says it this way. "You shall receive power of the kind, which God has and exerts."[43] WOW! Jesus told his followers just before he left, "I am going to send you what my Father has promised; but stay in the city *until you have been clothed with power from on high*."[44] When the Holy Spirit fell on

me in the shadowy confines of that tent, I was clothed with power!
In fact, *I was supercharged!*

Taking Issue

In the first place, I hear that when you come together as a church,
there are divisions among you, and to some extent I believe it.
No doubt there have to be differences among you
to show which of you have God's approval.
(1 Corinthians 11:18-19)

The man who thinks he knows something does
not yet know as he ought to know.
(1 Corinthians 8:2)

There's been a lot of senseless debate about the ministry
of the Holy Spirit. The dispute seems to boil down to one major
issue—tongues. Many well-meaning saints have embraced it as
their own pet doctrine and have made it an issue of divisiveness!

Unfortunately, to many this doctrine is not so much a tool
to use in their devotional life, it has become a weapon. A weapon
to strike at other Christians, whom they do not consider to be
Spirit-filled, simply because their experience was not exactly like
theirs. In addition, they tend to view the Holy Spirit as something
of a lever used to lift them up above those brothers and sisters.
"Yes, we're the ones with God's approval! After all, *we* speak in
tongues!" How it must sadden God's heart when we allow such
arrogance into our hearts.

You may be thinking, "Ah-h-h! You're just saying that
because you don't believe in the gift of tongues!" WRONG! Then
you may wondering, "Does the *Rodster* speak in tongues?' Well,

how shall I answer you? Is the Pope Catholic?! Yes, I certainly do pray in the spirit in an unknown language during my daily private devotions.

Paul said. "For anyone who speaks in a tongue does not speak to men but to God. Indeed, no one understands him; he utters mysteries with his spirit."[45] I love having this blessing in my prayer life! I figure that if it was good enough for the Apostle Paul, it's definitely good enough for me. However, and listen carefully to this; *when it comes to the filling of the Holy Spirit, the issue is not tongues — the issue is truth and power.*

The Reason for the Infilling of the Holy Spirit

> *"But when He, the Spirit of truth, comes,*
> *He will guide you into all truth.*
> — Jesus (John 16:13)

A father and his small son went fishing. While they were out in the boat, the boy did what little boys often do—ask questions...

How does this boat float?

The father replied, *"Don't rightly know son."*

A little later, the boy looked at his father and asked, *"How do fish breathe underwater?"*

Once again the father replied, *"Don't rightly know son."*

A little later the boy asked his father, *"Why is the sky blue?"*

Again, the father replied. *"Don't rightly know son."*

Finally, the boy asked his father, *"Dad, do you mind my asking you all of these questions?"*

The father replied, *"Of course not, son, you'll never learn anything if you don't ask questions."*

In my continuing quest for truth, I have endeavored to study this subject as thoroughly as possible, and I still continue to do so. One thing I discovered early in my search was that, like the father in the story, *I don't have all of the answers*. However, I have arrived at a few conclusions that I feel are worth the prayerful consideration of those who have the same love for truth that I have. If you think that my deductions are misguided, I trust that the Holy Spirit, who leads us into all truth, will point out my error. It wouldn't be the first time! This ol' boy needs a *lot* of guidance.

First, I believe one can be filled with the Holy Spirit and never speak in an unknown tongue. "How can you say such a thing, Rod?" you may ask. Well, once you've trudged through the traditional teachings of men it becomes fairly simple to arrive at this reasoning. If we all practice one of the less popular attributes of the fruit of the Spirit called *patience,* I will try to explain myself.

I have searched the scripture from glossary to maps and have yet to find any *teaching* in the entire Bible that asserts that unknown tongues is the foremost evidence of the infilling of the Holy Spirit. I'm sorry my Pentecostal/Charismatic friend. Bear in mind that I am one of you. I love you dearly and I mean you no offence, but it is just not there—*as a doctrine*. This is tantamount to the line of reasoning I wish to present concerning this matter. Again, the Bible does not clearly *present* speaking in tongues as the only evidence that one has been filled with the Holy Spirit, but perhaps should be considered rather a consequence of the filling.

"You have let go of the commands of God and are holding on to the traditions of men." — Jesus (Mark 7:8)

To the Jews who had believed him, Jesus said,
"If you hold to my teaching, you are really my disciples.
Then you will know the truth and the truth will set you free."
— Jesus (John 8:31-32)

Please, don't misunderstand. I'm not trying to make an argument *against* tongues. As I have already stated this wonderful blessing is part of my prayer life. Why would I argue against it? I'm simply trying, in my own clumsy way, to cut through some old moldy traditional teachings of men on this subject and get to the truth. So, please bear with me.

Note that Jesus didn't say that truth in and of itself will set you free. He said it is the *personal knowledge* of the truth that sets one free. The Greek word for "know" used here is "to know by experience and observation"[46] It's not enough just to have an intellectual knowledge of the truth; one must embrace it and hold onto to it. Only then will one experience true freedom.

Many teach that speaking in an unknown tongue is the evidence of the infilling of the Holy Spirit. The base for such an assumption is primarily taken from accounts recorded in *The Acts of the Apostles*, where chapter two gives the account of the early disciples speaking in tongues when they were "filled" with the Holy Spirit. However, using this passage to claim that one must speak in tongues as proof that they have received the infilling of the Holy Spirit is based mainly upon assumptions and the traditions of men. When you prayerfully read the other accounts found in Acts you'll discovery that there are many reports of people being filled by the Holy Spirit without any mention of speaking in tongues.

Examining the Evidence

Take the Holy Spirit's comming upon Jesus at the Jordan River for instance.[47] The Holy Spirit fell on him in the form of a dove. Furthermore, there is no mention of our Lord speaking in tongues when it happened. As a matter of fact the only *heavenly language* anyone heard that day was a voice from Heaven saying, "This is my Son, whom I love; with him I am well pleased."[48]

Another example is the Apostle Paul. What took place when he was filled with the Holy Spirit? As you recall the Lord sent a Godly, if somewhat reluctant, man named Ananias to go and meet with Paul who was then called Saul.

> *Then Ananias went to the house and entered it. Placing his hands on Saul, he said, "Brother Saul, the Lord Jesus, who appeared to you on the road as you were coming here has sent me so that you may see again **and be filled with the Holy Spirit.**" Immediately, something like scales fell from Saul's eyes, and he could see again. He got up and was baptized.*   (Acts 9:17-18)

Notice there's no mention of Paul speaking in tongues on this occassion. You can read it into the account if you want, but it is simply not there. I know that many insist that he did based on what happened to the believers in Acts chapter two. Plus, when you consider the fact that the Apostle Paul wrote more about tongues than any other New Testament writer, it's understandable that some would make such an assumption. Unfortunately, making assumptions is one way many of us maintain a strong *death grip* on our deeply embedded traditions.

Please, hear me out. I promise that I have a pure motive behind what I'm saying. Please know that *my intention is not to offend but to enlighten.* And by so doing, I want to hopefully pull down one of the many walls that have divided God's people.

The Danger of Making Assumptions

"Some minds are like concrete,
thoroughly mixed up and permanently set."
—unknown

Now, if you insist on maintaining that someone is not *Spirit-filled* simply because they did not speak in tongues the way that the disciples did on the day of Pentecost, then consider this. In light of this same assumption could it be that you have not been filled with the Holy Spirit either?

When the day of Pentecost came, they were all together in one place. Suddenly a sound like the blowing of a violent wind came from heaven and filled the whole house where they were sitting. They saw what seemed to be tongues of fire that separated and came to rest on each of them. All of them were filled with the Holy Spirit and began to speak in other tongues as the Spirit enabled them. (Acts 2:1-4)

If you make these four verses the primary basis of your entire theology concerning Spiritual baptism and then argue that this is the way you get *it* or you don't have *it,* then please follow that argument all the way through to it's obvious conclusion. *You're not filled either!* Let me explain.

When you experienced the infilling of the Holy Spirit was the room filled with "a sound like the blowing of a violent wind?" Did visible "tongues of fire" descend from Heaven and rest on you? And when all this happened, did other nationalities clearly hear you speaking in their native language?

Most importantly, did you then go out to the streets and start preaching the Gospel with such power and boldness that thousands of people were saved? This is extremely important because this is the significant "why" of the filling of the Holy Spirit. Incredibly, many who claim to be *Spirit-filled* don't have nerve enough to witness to a cat! More about this later.

Consider this if you will, some accounts given in the book of Acts say that some spoke in tongues *and* prophesied[49], while others just prophesied without any mention of tongues.[50] I mean no offence when I ask you this, but during your experience did you prophesy? Did all these manifestation occur when you were filled with the Holy Spirit? Did you say, *"No.?* Well, I'm sorry, my friend, but based on your own line of reasoning you have never received the infilling of the Holy Spirit.

A Warning from a Former Critic

Wait a minute! Don's get out the pompoms and start cheering just yet. I would like to address the other extreme as well, if I may. And I will because, after all *it's my book!*

Please, heed some advice from one critic who used to make value judgments about *the "pentecostals."* I would see them on the TV from time to time or hear one on the radio. I mocked and ridiculed them to the point of my own embarrassment. [Not to their face; that takes too much nerve] I would refer to anyone with Pentecostal or Charismatic leanings as a bunch of nuts. Guess what? Now, I'm one of the nuts! Don't you just love God's wonderful sense of irony?

I am dreadfully ashamed of the way I behaved. I was blindly stepping way out of bounds by setting myself up as a bastion of all truth. My spiritual arrogance led me to ignore scriptural admonitions such as, *"Who are you to judge someone else's servant? To his own master he stands or falls. And he will stand, for the Lord is able to make him stand." "Therefore let us stop passing judgment on one another. Instead, make up your mind not to put any stumbling block or obstacle in your brother's way."* [51]

Finally, all of you, live in harmony with one another; be sympathetic, love as brothers, be compassionate and humble.
(1 Peter 3:8)

The goal of this command is love, which comes from a pure heart and a good conscience and a sincere faith. Some have wandered away from these and turned to meaningless talk. (1 Timothy 1:5-6)

My brothers and sisters, why do we battle over secondary doctrinal issues? Paul wrote about divisive issues in the early church and clearly pointed to what the real focus should be. *"For in Christ Jesus neither circumcision nor uncircumcision* [any secondary issue] *has any value. **The only thing that counts is faith expressing itself through love."*** [52] That's the bottom line. God is more concerned with how well we express love toward one another than he is about whether or not we hold to a particular doctrine. Jesus settled the issue of what is the true evidence of being filled by the Holy Spirit with this simple statement. *"By this all men will know that you are my disciples, if you love one another."* [53]

My friend, if you are guilty of judging other believers over this or any other doctrinal issue then I will ask you the same question I asked my judgmental self; "Rod, when did God retire and leave you in charge?"

*There is only one Lawgiver and Judge, the one who is able to save and destroy. **But you who are you to judge your neighbor?*** (James 4:12)

The Do's and the Don'ts

In the same way, the Spirit helps us in our weakness. We do not know what we ought to pray for, but the Spirit himself intercedes for us with groans that words cannot express. (Romans 8:26)

And pray in the Spirit on all occasions with all kinds of prayers and requests. (Ephesians 6:18a)

I am grateful for my prayer language. It is a wonderful blessing that God offers Christians to help in their prayer life. However, if you choose not to accept this blessing, then that is strictly between you and *your* Master. My intention is not to present some long drawn out argument for a particular teaching. No, not at all. Neither do I wish to imply in any way that you are something of a second-class citizen in the Kingdom of God if you do not pray the same as I do. If that is what you are reading into this you are missing my heart by a long shot.

My concern is simple. My evangelical friend, please don't let "Tongues?! We-dun-need-no-steen-king-tongues!" keep you from enjoying the rich fellowship of other believers. Too many sweet saints, who pray in an unknown tongue, have been ostracized from denominations by those who don't. Even though God's word is crystal clear when it says, *"...do not forbid speaking in tongues."* [54]

But the fruit of the Spirit is love, joy, peace, patience, kindness, goodness, faithfulness, gentleness and self-control.
Against such things there is no law.
(Galatians 5: 22-23)

As for my Pentecostal/Charismatic brothers and sisters, you too have been just as guilty of spiritual elitism. I therefore offer this caution. *Please, don't be guilty of being tongue-tied! In other words, don't become so tied to the **gifts** that you forget about the **fruit** of the Spirit. The most important of which is love.* Be very careful lest you are found guilty of snubbing your nose at other believers just because they do not believe exactly as you do about the ministry of the Holy Spirit.

Getting Down to the Real Issue

"A new command I give you: Love one another.
*As I have loved you, so you **must** love one another.*
By this all men will know that you are my disciples,
if you love one another." — Jesus (John 13:34-35)

Dear friends, let us love one another, for love comes from God.
Everyone who loves has been born of God and knows God.
(1John 4:7)

Why must we fuss over something for which none of us
have all the answers? Why do we insist on breaking fellowship
over *any* issue, short of immorality or outrageous heresy, for that
matter? As a friend of mine once said, "There's going to be a lot
of surprises when we all get to heaven." How true! It will be an
eye opening experience for all of us. Therefore consider this; it is
far better to go amiss in one's secondary theological views then to
fall short in one's love for other believers. *May God help me to be
a lover of the saints and not a theological lawyer.*

Love cannot be defined.
It can only be described and demonstrated.

The original Greek word, that Jesus uses in his command
to *love* one another, is *agapeo*. It is the verb form of *agape*.
Vine's says "Love [agape] can be known only from the actions
it prompts."[55] Vine goes on the say, "Christian love, whether
exercised toward the brethren, or toward men generally, is not an
impulse from the feelings, it does not always run with the natural
inclinations, nor does it spend itself only upon those for whom
some affinity is discovered."[54] In other words *agape* is love with
legs on it. It is a love that is *not* driven by tender affection, but
rather, is inspired by obedience to God. You don't feel *agape*. You
do *agape*.[56]

If I speak in the tongues of men and of angels, but have not love,
I am only a resounding gong or a clanging cymbal.
(1Corinthians 13:1)

To our shame, so many of our so-called "Full Gospel Churches" are empty of what really matters. They are full of a lot of noise and hype, but sadly lacking in love and acceptance of other believers. Jesus said that love is the most important quality the Church possesses. It is one of the things that bind us together. Jesus commanded us to, above all else, love one another. *He said that it' is the one recognizable manifestation that marks us as Christians.* He did not say it was whether or not operate in the spiritual gifts. Jesus did not say it was how knowledgeable we are about the Bible that defined us, or how well we adhered to some religious code of ethics. He said that love for one another sets us apart from the rest of the world!

> *"If anyone loves me, he will obey my teaching.*
> *My Father will love him, and we will come to him*
> *and make our home with him. He who does not love me*
> *will not obey my teaching. These words you hear are*
> *not my own; they belong to the Father who sent me."*
> — Jesus (John 14:23-24)

Furthermore, Jesus didn't say, "A new *suggestion* I give you... " It was a command from our King! He did not tell us to safeguard our particular religious creeds or practices. Nor did he say to pull away from, or criticize, those believers with whom we disagree. Jesus said to love each other with complete abandonment and acceptance, just like he loves us. And if we truly love him, we will obey him.

> *Whoever loves his brother lives in the light, and*
> *there is nothing in him to make him stumble.*
> (1John 2:10)

A Return when He Returns

"*Again, [the Kingdom of Heaven] will be like a man going on a journey, who called his servants and entrusted his property to them. To one he gave five talents*[57] *of money, to another two talents, and to another one talent, each according to his ability. Then he went on his journey. The man who had received the five talents went at once and put his money to work and gained five more. So also, the one with the two talents gained two more.* **But the man who had received the one talent went off, dug a hole in the ground and hid his master's money***.*

"*After a long time the master of those servants returned and settled accounts with them. The man who had received the five talents brought the other five. 'Master,' he said, 'you entrusted me with five talents. See, I have gained five more.' His master replied, 'Well done, good and faithful servant! You have been faithful with a few things; I will put you in charge of many things. Come and share your master's happiness!'*

"*The man with the two talents also came. 'Master,' he said, 'you entrusted me with two talents; see, I have gained two more.' His master replied, 'Well done, good and faithful servant! You have been faithful with a few things; I will put you in charge of many things. Come and share your master's happiness!'*

"*Then the man who had received the one talent came. 'Master,' he said, 'I knew that you are a hard man, harvesting where you have not sown and gathering where you have not scattered seed. So I was afraid and went out and hid your talent in the ground. See, here is what belongs to you' His master replied, 'You wicked, lazy servant! So you knew that I harvest where I have not sown and gather where I have not scattered seed? Well then, you should have put my money on deposit with the bankers, so that when I returned I would have received it back with interest. Take the talent from him and give it to the one who has the ten talents. For everyone who has will be given more, and he will have an abundance. Whoever does not have, even what he has will be taken from him."*— Jesus (Matthew 25:14-29)

I could be totally wrong about the spiritual gifts controversy but, then again, so could you. As the old song goes, "We will understand it better bye and bye."[58] However, this one thing I *do* know. I believe the day has arrived that the Lord is now calling his Church on the carpet. He has made some major *investments* in us. It would seem that Spirit-filled believers have been gifted beyond measure and for a good reason. Now, God's looking at us and demanding a return on his investments.

"From everyone who has been given much, much will be demanded; and from the one who has been entrusted with much, much more will be asked." — Jesus (Luke 12:48)

God is seeking a return from his investment in us. He is not in the least interested in how well we have protected our little pet doctrines. *No, God is not impressed with how well we have hidden, or guarded, the gifts with which he has blessed us. He wants to know what we're doing with those blessings!*

God expects results! Our master *will* return one day and when he does he will expect a yield. "How many souls have you won?" he'll ask us. "How many lives are better because of you? What have you done with the gifts I've given you?" Jesus could not care less about our intensely guarded belief systems. "Have you carried out the commission I've giving you? That's why I gave the baptism of the Holy Spirit. It was to empower you to reach the lost. Have you done that?" This is what concerns the Master and good answers will not be sufficient at the Judgment!

Many, however, are like the foolish servant who wasted his valuable time, resources, and energy protecting his little gift. Instead of using it he carefully buried it in the ground. I can imagine him taking it out from time to time and holding it, cherishing it. He may even have looked at it admiringly and thought to himself, "Boy, look what the master gave me. Isn't it cool?! I bet those other two guys don't have a gift as good as mine."

Sadly, he was found wanting when the master returned. Why? Because he did not value and utilize what the master gave him. Thus, he had no increase to offer. Look at what the master called him. *"You wicked, lazy servant!"* Is this how God views those of us who don't use the gifts he gave us—wicked and lazy? The master's only recourse was to take what this servant had and give it to the one producing the greatest results. [Those of us who call ourselves Spirit-filled should take serious warning from this parable, for God in these last days is already spreading his gifts across denominational lines]

Gifts or Investments?

"From everyone who has been given much, much will be demanded; and from the one who has been entrusted with much, much more will be asked. "— Jesus
(Luke 12:48)

The foolish servant failed to see the *why* behind what the master gave him and therefore didn't put it to work. Too many of us Charismatics/Pentecostals are the same way. We do not see the gifts of the Spirit as they really are—the *investments* of the Spirit. Instead of using the gifts as tools to edify one another and to reach the world through a powerful, supernatural, display of the preaching of Gospel, we hoard them. Many, like little children, make toys of them to be played with and admired. Others of us use the gifts of the Holy Spirit as a gage to judge who they think is the most spiritual. God forgive us!

Let me offer another word about unity while we are looking at this passage. Consider this possibility; imagine the yield that the three servants could have offered their returning master if they had worked together. Now, think of the harvest we could offer our Lord if all those who profess to know him would lay aside their differences and started pooling the resources God has given us!

Think of it! A spiritual D-Day where believers from all over the world put away pettiness and unite with one common goal—to see the world's lost and dying set free! Wow! May I suggest that while we await *our* Master's return that we work together. Let's combine the resources with which God has provided all believers and, together, reach out to as many people as we can before it's too late. Let's spare one another the "friendly fire" and turn our guns on the real enemy—those evil forces that have our family members, friends, and the people of the world bound in darkness.

But, Rod, those other churches don't baptize in water the same way we do!

Well considering water baptism, though very important, is still just a visual representation of an inward spiritual experience.[59] *So, what difference does it make? Do they preach the true gospel?*

Well, yes … but they don't worship on the same day we do.

Considering the fact that every day is the Lord's Day[60]*, what is your point? I ask again, are they preaching the true gospel?*

But they don't do things the way we do them or believe the same way we believe about certain things.

For starters, if salvation is by grace and not by personal effort,[61] *then the ways in which different denominations worship God is totally between them and their Master. It, therefore, has no effect on their righteous standing with God. And as far as their secondary doctrinal viewpoints go, if they preach the true gospel, what difference does it make? Unless, of course, you're like I use to be, someone who acted as if he was the harbinger or all truth and wisdom.*

> *"My prayer is not for them alone. I pray also for those*
> *who will believe in me through their message,*
> ***that all of them may be one, Father, just as you are***
> ***in me and I am in you. May they also be in us***
> ***so that the world may believe that you have sent me."***
> — Jesus (John 17:20-21)

This prayer clearly reveals the heart of our LORD concerning his followers. Now, the question is this. Does the yearning that filled Jesus' heart fill our hearts as well? Do we desire to be one with other believers in much the same way that Christ is one with the Father? Please don't misunderstand, I'm not saying that we should all become one corporately, but rather become one in heart and purpose. We can fulfill Jesus' longing but only if we repent of religious arrogance, pull down the walls that have separated us, and then embrace one another as Christ commanded us.[62]

If anyone says, "I love God," yet hates his brother, he is a liar. For anyone who does not love his brother, whom he has seen, cannot love God, whom he has not seen. And **he has given us this** **command***: Whoever loves God must also love his brother.*
(1John 4:20-21)

If you really keep the royal law found in Scripture, "Love your neighbor as yourself," you are doing right. But if you show favoritism, you sin and are convicted by the law as lawbreakers.
(James 2:8-9)

I'm not trying to offend any of my fellow believers and I certainly mean no disrespect. There's nothing wrong with being part a church, or denomination, where you feel God has placed you. Part of being free in Christ is to have your own opinion on doctrinal issues. However, having an opinion is one thing, being intolerant of other Christians' right to have their opinion is something else. Being opinionated to the point of divisiveness and religious bigotry is not reflecting the heart of Christ. It is not obeying his command to "love one another"[63].

I'm convinced that the greatest source of division in the

Body of Christ is caused by sincere, Bible loving, believers who choose to think with their brain rather than with their heart. They, therefore, focus on the differences they see rather than on the commonality that all true believers share. We must realize that we all have a shared aim—reaching the world for Christ. There will never be a spiritual D-Day until we lay aside secondary differences and unite as one in spirit and in heart.

> *... so in Christ we who are many form one body,*
> *and each member belongs to all the others.*
> (Romans 12:5)

> *The body is a unit, though it is made up of many parts;*
> *and though all its parts are many, they form one body.*
> *So it is with Christ.*
> (1 Corinthians 12:12)

"Where's the Beef?" Reason for Ministry of the Holy Spirit

Now, a few concluding comments about the tongues/gifts controversy before moving on. Again I say that I believe one can be filled with the Holy Spirit without uttering unknown tongues. [Please, don't miss this] But at the same time, one can also speak in tongues having never been filled with the Holy Spirit! Let me explain. I know of many [and so do you] who profess to be "Spirit-filled" with all the utterances, yet they have no heart to reach the lost. Furthermore, their lives display very little, if any, of God's love and power! They are big about displaying the *gifts* but demonstrate little of the *fruit* of the Spirit.

> *"Thus, by their fruit you will recognize them."* — Jesus
> (Matthew 7:20)

"But you will receive power when the Holy Spirit comes on you;
and you will be my witnesses in Jerusalem, and in all Judea and
Samaria, and to the ends of the earth." — Jesus (Acts 1:8)

Jesus proclaimed that one of the primary ministries of the Holy Spirit was to *clothe* us with power for witnessing. Please, don't tell folks that you are filled with God's Holy Spirit just because you display some *gift*. Let's see some boldness in witnessing to the lost. Let's see the people your life has touched, please. Where are the souls you've brought to Jesus? Or as the little old lady[64] used to say in the classic Wendy's Hamburger commercials, "Where's the beef?!" Oh yes, you can be baptized with the Holy Spirit without the initial evidence of speaking in tongues. However, you will *never* prove to the world that you are Spirit-filled without demonstrating a passion for the lost and a powerful display of boldness in winning them for Christ!

Stanley Squeamish Becomes a Lion

When I was filled with the Holy Spirit on that summer day in 1965, I was saturated with a holy boldness that I had never known before. I went nuts! My friends nearly freaked! They didn't know what to make of me. Stanley Squeamish, the spiritual wimp that they all knew and loved, went home for the summer but a roaring lion returned to school the following fall. I went fanatical on everyone! It was a scary thing! I had become a wild-eyed, golden-hearted, wall-climbing, Bible-thumping, fully rational minded fanatic!

But if I say, "I will not mention Him
or speak any more in His name,"

His word is in my heart like a fire, a fire shut up in my bones.
I am weary of holding it in; indeed, I cannot.
(Jeremiah 20:9)

No one had to guess where *I* stood on spiritual matters. I made no bones about my love for the Lord. It wasn't long before I ran most of my old friends off. I could not keep silent about Jesus, which is a condition I haven't been able to get over since.

That's what being filled with the Holy Spirit will do for you. You'll become a spiritual chatterbox, so full of God that it becomes like fire shut up in your bones. You'll try to win your friends, your family, and your neighbors. Why, you might even find yourself witnessing to the dog if he'll listen. Now, *that's* being filled with the Holy Spirit! Anything else is a wrong skirt dragging you away from God's call and purpose for your life.

7

THE 'FAITH-GOD' SKIRT

The Gospel Of Greed And
Other Small Idols

W e go to seminar after seminar that teaches us how to get stuff from God.

You were running a good race. Who cut in on you and kept you from obeying the truth?

(Galatians 5: 7)

I feel I must offer one final word of caution concerning the gifts of the Holy Spirit before continuing. Be careful, my "Spirit-filled" brothers and sisters, lest you do what that child in the narrative at the beginning of this book did. He was distracted from his mother by toys. You too could find yourself distracted from the course God has set for you by the glitter of toys. Many in the Charismatic/ Pentecostal movement have released their grip on the fundamental principles that birthed this great Spiritual revival and have chased after toys. *We have sought the gifts rather than the Gift-Giver.*

*On reaching Jerusalem, Jesus entered the temple area and began driving out those who were buying and selling there. He overturned the tables of the money changers and the benches of those selling doves, and would not allow anyone to carry merchandise through the temple courts. And as he taught them, he said, "Is it not written: "'My house will be called a house of prayer for all nations'? But **you have made it 'a den of robbers**." "* (Mark 11:15-17)

Some years ago I was attending a worship services at a church where a friend of mine attended. The guest "preacher' that night was a well known "faith and prosperity teacher." At the end of the praise and worship segment the pastor gave the floor to him. What happened next sickened me to the core.

The guest stood before the audience and began to speak. "God has directed me lately to do something I've been doing for pastors, and I'm going to do it tonight." He asked the pastor to stand in front of the congregation. He then directed his attention back at the audience and said, "God told me to tell you to come forward and lay money at your pastor's feet." Then, he began to relate incidents where he had done this before and claimed he saw pastors standing in a pile of money up to their knees, waist band, and even some pastors had a pile of money surrounding up to their shoulders.

Then he came in for the kill. "God told me to tell you that there's a hundredfold blessing tonight on everyone who comes forward and lays money at this pastor's feet. Note: the offering was for the pastor to keep. "There's a hundredfold blessing on your offering when you bring your money up here tonight!" he reiterated. "So give your best 'seed' offering and God will bless your 'seed' a hundredfold!"

I watched as person after person blindly came forward, without question or pause, and laid money on the floor at the pastor's feet. "Yes, keep coming!" he continued. "Don't miss out on the hundredfold blessing God has for you." I sat in stunned silence, as if watching a lioness stalk and bring down her prey on Animal Planet. I could stand it no longer. I got out of my seat and hurried out of there. When I got home I felt like I needed a shower after witnessing that shameful display of sheep shearing.

"John 19 tells us that Jesus wore designer clothes. Well, what else you gonna call it? 'Designer clothes–that's blasphemy.' No, that's what we call them today. I mean, you didn't get the stuff he wore off the rack. It wasn't a one-size-fits-all deal. No, this was custom stuff. It was the kind of a garment that kings and rich merchants wore. Kings and rich merchants wore that garment…You don't think these Apostles didn't walk around with money? I mean, they had money. I just thank God that I saw this and gave up the denominational line and got on God's line before I starved me and all my family to death. Go to Acts 24. 1 mean, you don't think there wasn't money in this Paul's life! … Paul had the kind of money that people, that government officials, would, would block up justice to try to get a bribe out of old Paul." [65]

"Jesus had a nice house, a big house - big enough to have company stay the night with Him at the house. Let me show you His house. Go over to John the first chapter and I'll show you His house.... Now, child of God, that's a house big enough to have company stay the night in. There's His house."[66]

"Foxes have holes and birds of the air have nests,
but the Son of Man has no place to lay his head."
— Jesus (Matthew 8:20)

Many years ago I went to Fort Worth, TX to attend a convention hosted by some well known *mega-faith* teachers. At that time my family and I attended a "Word of Faith" Church, and at our pastor's insistence, we attended the event. Looking back I realize that God was behind my decision to go because he wanted to open my eyes about the excesses in the whole "word of faith" "prosperity" message.

During one afternoon session I sat in the balcony studying what was happening on the floor below. What I saw and heard that day left an indelible image on my mind. To this day it sickens me when I think of it.

The speaker for the afternoon, was one of the regular teachers at these conventions. When he spoke I found out why.

Back during my "word of faith" phase, I used to regularly watch
the promoter of this event on TV and listened to his teachings on
cassette. Often I heard him refer to this man as "God's banker."
However, this erroneous message offers not only one of greed, but
it's greed with a self-promoting purpose. [67]

"Poverty is not an accident, and neither is
prosperity. Strict spiritual laws govern both. The spiritual
law of release says be willing to release for increase. 'There
is that scattereth, and yet increaseth; and there is [he] that
withholdeth more than is meet, but it tendeth to poverty. The
liberal soul shall be made fat: and he that watereth shall be
watered himself.'[68] Many of you haven't tithed in years and
God's word says that there is curse on anyone who doesn't
give their tithes and offerings."

He continued on in this vain for about forty-five
minutes and then he went in for the kill. "'The liberal soul
shall be made fat: and he that watereth shall be watered
himself.'" He repeated. "You want God to prosper you, to
make you debt free, but this is not going to happen because
you are robbing God of his tithes and offerings. Malachi 3:8
says, 'Will a man rob God? Yet ye have robbed me. But ye
say, 'Wherein have we robbed thee? In tithes and offerings."

He continued this brazen show of master manipulation.
"Then verse nine says," he continued. "Ye are cursed with
a curse for ye have robbed me, even this whole nation."
You see, my brothers and sisters, you are living under a
curse! God won't open the windows of Heaven until you do
something that will break that curse. Now, how do you break
that curse? Verse ten and eleven tells us how. 'Bring ye all

the tithes into the storehouse, that there may be meat in mine house, and prove me now herewith, saith the LORD of hosts, if I will not open you the windows of heaven, and pour you out a blessing, that there shall not be room enough to receive it. And I will rebuke the devourer for your sakes, and he shall not destroy the fruits of your ground; neither shall your vine cast her fruit before the time in the field, saith the LORD of hosts."[69]

"Prove me," God says. Break the curse over your finances. 'How do I do that, brother John?' you say." Then the preacher went for the jugular. "Here's how; get out your checkbook right now and write out the *biggest* curse breaking check you've ever written!" I watched as people all over the building opened their pocketbooks and wallets. "Now, get up from your seats and bring your seed offering to the altar." he said.

And they did just that. By the hundreds they went forward, cash and checks in hand, and dropped money into the offering buckets setting on the floor up front. Then when I thought he couldn't act more shameless, he stood facing the crowd with arms outstretched to his side in the sign of a cross. Then, as if he were the Pope or something, he began saying,

"You're forgiven in Jesus name! That's right keep coming, children. You're forgiven in Jesus name! The curse is broken! You're forgiven in Jesus name!" Again and again he repeated the mantra, and the buckets filled to overflow with the spoils collected from those trusting saints.

I soon realized that this afternoon session was chiefly designed to sheer the sheep. This man's lecture on giving had little

to do with encouraging the listeners to give their tithe to the local
church where they attended, which is where it belongs. But rather
this "message" was presented in order to help fill the coffers of
their "ministries.

"There is somebody watching that recently came into some
money. You need to call in a tithe on it." [70]

*Unlike so many, **we do not peddle the word of God for profit**.*
On the contrary, in Christ we speak before God
with sincerity, like men sent from God.
(2 Corinthians 2:17)

Prosperity preachers, take scriptures like Malachi chapter
three completely out of context. Their purpose is to manipulate
people into giving their tithes, which is to go "into the storehouse
(their home church)" and offerings, which one gives outside
of the tithe. Note: the offering should be given after prayerful
consideration to determine where God wants it to go. It is NOT to
be given for the purpose of getting financial gain from God. But
these Prosperity predators want it all for themselves. In fact, they
are embezzling from God by taking money that rightfully should
go the local church.

*"If anyone would come after me, he **must deny himself***
and take up his cross and follow me. —Jesus (Matthew 16:24)

We go to seminar after seminar that teaches us how to
get stuff from God. We then sit for hours on end listening to these
so-called "faith teachers" tell us how to be healthy, wealthy, and
wise, rather than teaching us how to develop the character of
Christ in our lives and how to win souls. It's not surprising that

there are so few world changers in the western church. Very few of us are willing to pay the price of true service. We've been taught this "bless-me" message for so long that we've lost sight of the cross. *We've become self-centered rather than others-centered.*

The excesses promoted in the "prosperity" message and the supposed "faith movement" have greatly helped to fuel this "What's in it for me?" mindset. The result is that we now have a generation of self-centered believers who have been programmed to think that one gives in order to get.

These false faith teachers con their audience with promises of financial freedom and prosperity to all those who give money to them. "There's a hundred fold blessing on this offering today. Make sure you give your very best 'seed offering', because God is going to really bless you when you do." *Whether we are aware it or not we've put conditions on our service to God and others.* In other words, we've been taught to give, not out of love and obedience to God, but in order to get financial gain from God. *Shame on us!*

If anyone teaches false doctrines and does not agree to the sound instruction of our Lord Jesus Christ and to godly teaching, he is conceited and understands nothing. He has an unhealthy interest in controversies and quarrels about words that result in envy, strife, malicious talk, evil suspicions and constant friction between men of corrupt mind, **who have been robbed of the truth and who think that godliness is a means to financial gain.**

But godliness with contentment is great gain. For we brought nothing into the world, and we can take nothing out of it. But if we have food and clothing, we will be content with

*that. People who want to get rich fall into temptation and a
trap and into many foolish and harmful desires that plunge men
into ruin and destruction. For the love of money is a root of all
kinds of evil. Some people, eager for money, have wandered
from the faith and pierced themselves with many griefs. But
you, man of God, **flee from all this, and pursue righteousness,
godliness, faith, love, endurance and gentleness***.

(1 Timothy 6:3-11)

More sad examples

"I'm telling you, Jesus wasn't poor, and He didn't wear no
rags, either. Like we march on these Easter little plays that we do
at our church, with those raggedy sheets on. Jesus didn't have no
rags on. He wore designer clothes, honey!"[72]

"The Word of God declares that we will not see 'the
righteous forsaken, nor his seed begging bread'.[71] All you have
to do today is sow your seed in faith and see what God will
do for you. As you sow your seed and claim the promises of
Genesis 26:12-19, pray that God's Spirit will anoint your seed
supernaturally. There is such a strong anointing on this word right
now for you to sow for your future as you plant your seed toward
the proclaiming of the Gospel.

As you pray over the amount of your seed that you are
sending today, ask God to touch your life supernaturally, just as
He touched Isaac's, even in the midst of famine and in spite of his
enemies. Ask God to anoint your income and unstop the wells in
your life that the enemy has plugged up. Ask the Lord to do for
you what He did for His servant Isaac. Believe Him today that as
you sow your seed, you, too, will receive a hundredfold harvest in

the same year. Do that and then send your offering by clicking on
DONATE NOW.   I, too, will pray and believe with you that the
Lord will do for you just what He promised!   I will be looking
for your seed so that I may agree with you that God will do for
you what He did for Isaac, His servant."[73]

As you read this passage to which this famous *Faith
Teacher* referred, notice that there are no promises from God in
it, much less promises of financial blessings to us! It is simply
a historical reference showing how God blessed Isaac. It is just
another example of how God's Word can be manipulated in a way
designed to separate you from your money.

> *Isaac planted crops in that land and the same year reaped
> a hundredfold, because the LORD blessed him. The man
> became rich, and his wealth continued to grow until he
> became very wealthy. He had so many flocks and herds and
> servants that the Philistines envied him. So all the wells
> that his father's servants had dug in the time of his father
> Abraham, the Philistines stopped up, filling them with earth.
> Then Abimelech said to Isaac, "Move away from us; you
> have become too powerful for us." So Isaac moved away
> from there and encamped in the Valley of Gerar and settled
> there. Isaac reopened the wells that had been dug in the time
> of his father Abraham, which the Philistines had stopped up
> after Abraham died, and he gave them the same names his
> father had given them. Isaac's servants dug in the valley and
> discovered a well of fresh water there.* (Genesis 26: 12-19)

> *"...who think that godliness is a means to financial gain."*

"What do you need? Start creating it. Start speaking about it. Start speaking it into being. Speak to your billfold. Say, 'You big, thick billfold full of money.' Speak to your checkbook. Say, 'You, checkbook, you. You've never been so prosperous since I owned you. You're just jammed full of money." [74]

"Some people, eager for money, have wandered from the faith."

"The whole point is I'm trying to get you to see–to get you out of this malaise of thinking that Jesus and the disciples were poor and then relating that to you – thinking that you, as a child of God, have to follow Jesus. The Bible says that He has left us an example that we should follow His steps. That's the reason why I drive a Rolls Royce. I'm following Jesus' steps." [75]

Keep your lives free from the love of money and be content with what you have, because God has said, "Never will I leave you; never will I forsake you."   (Hebrews 13:5)

In the same way, any of you who does not give up everything he has cannot be my disciple. – Jesus   (Luke 14:33)

Many in this movement have changed the relationship they had with God from servant to LORD, to employee to employer. They no longer serve or give out of love for the God who redeemed them, but rather they serve with an attitude of one expecting wages. "Okay, I've given. Now, God *must* give it back, *plus more...* in Jesus name!" God forgive us!

But there were also false prophets among the people, just as there will be false teachers among you. They will secretly introduce destructive heresies, even denying the sovereign Lord who bought them — bringing swift destruction on themselves. Many will follow their shameful ways and will bring the way of truth into disrepute. ***In their greed these teachers will exploit you with stories they have made up.*** *Their condemnation has long been hanging over them, and their destruction has not been sleeping.* (2 Peter 2:1-3)

Losing Our Focus

"You say, [You confess] 'I am rich; I have acquired wealth and do not need a thing.' But you do not realize that you are wretched, pitiful, poor, blind and naked." — Jesus (Revelations 3:17)

"You shall not misuse the name of the LORD your God,
for the LORD will not hold anyone guiltless
who misuses His name."
— God, The Third Commandment (Exodus 20:7)

We've been taught to worship faith rather than the Faith-Giver. "I'm just speaking my faith, brother. I am rich and prosperous... *in Jesus name!*" Talk about misusing the Lord's name! Please don't misunderstand, I firmly believe that God wants to bless his people and he certainly honors faith. However, the focus of contemporary Charisma is a far cry from the toil and selflessness that birthed it. *The Christians whom the Holy Spirit fell on at Azusa Street were not seeking what God could do for them. They were seeking God!* We must regain our focus if this

Holy Spirit renewal is to survive. Indeed, it may be dead already.

> *In the year that King Uzziah died, I saw the Lord*
> *seated on a throne, high and exalted, and the train of his*
> *robe filled the temple. Above him were seraphs, each with*
> *six wings: With two wings they covered their faces, with two*
> *they covered their feet, and with two they were flying. And*
> *they were calling to one another: "Holy, holy, holy is the*
> *LORD Almighty; the whole earth is full of his glory."*
> *At the sound of their voices the doorposts and*
> *thresholds shook and the temple was filled with smoke. Woe*
> *to me!" I cried. "I am ruined! For I am a man of unclean*
> *lips, and I live among a people of unclean lips, and my eyes*
> *have seen the King, the LORD Almighty."* (Isaiah 6:1-5)

This generation of "Spirit filled" believers [indeed all believers] is in crucial need of an Isaiah experience. Our focus has been on *skirt grabbing* for so long that, somewhere in the hustle and bustle of hyper-spiritual hyperactivity, we've lost sight of our true focus — God. Our attention has been diverted by the glitter of toys. We've released our hold on the Gift-giver and have clung to the gifts. We profess that we have a firm grip on God... *but do we?* We think that we *know* him... *but do we?*

We've replaced a pure reverence for Holy God with a reverence for man, his movements, organizations, and pet doctrines. We've forgotten that our God is Holy, and when that happens we become vulnerable to excesses. We then become easy prey to deception. We then begin to look to men as a source of what to believe rather than prayerfully studying God's Word for ourselves. We then begin to raise T.V. preachers and gospel singers to the status of superstar when we forget that our God is Holy.

We become smug, spiritual elitists and even shun the fellowship of other Christians because "They don't have it like we do". We pick and choose when obeying scriptural edicts, when we forget that our God is Holy. Most importantly, we lose sight of the deficit in our own character and forget how desperately we need *God's* righteousness when we forget that OUR GOD IS HOLY!

Forgetting to Remember

"Yet I hold this against you: You have forsaken your first love. **Remember the height from which you have fallen! Repent and do the things you did at first.** *If you do not repent, I will come to you and remove your lampstand from its place."* — Jesus (Revelations 2:4-5)

Many of our once great Charismatic and Pentecostal churches that started out as mighty healing centers and soul winning stations have evolved into little more than a three-ring circus. Why? It's because we've lost our first love, our passion for knowing God and our zeal for winning souls. What is the Lord's response to our neglect? It's right here in this passage. He tells us it's time to *remember, repent and return. "But you will receive power when the Holy Spirit comes on you; and you will be my witnesses in Jerusalem, and in all Judea and Samaria, and to the ends of the earth."* —Jesus (Acts 1:8)

REMEMBER our spiritual roots. Remember why God gave us the Holy Spirit to begin with—to empower us for witnessing. Then we must **REPENT** of our pride and foolish behavior—the squandering of the precious gifts God gave us. We must then *RETURN* to the basics that birth this great, earth shaking movement—fervent prayer, selflessness, and an overwhelming hunger for God!

What has caused this great move of God to erode into what it is today? What happened to our momentum? What shipwrecked this dynamic revival that exploded in southern California in 1904? It was a revival of such magnitude that it swept across this nation, setting America ablaze with Holy Ghost fire. Tens of thousands were being saved and delivered on a national scale.[76]

What went wrong? It went from a movement to a fad and then became church denominations with their labels, or skirts. It was taken from the streets and put behind walls built by men. Then it began to lose steam. The fire started to diminish. The movement went into a tailspin from which they either couldn't or *wouldn't* pull out.

Then the late 1960's and early 1970's gave rise to the Jesus Movement[77] which in turn birthed the Charismatic renewal. This ushered in a fresh move of God that staggered America. Charismatic churches began to spring up all over the world. Mighty evangelistic centers were birthed everywhere as God's precious Holy Spirit began to once again sweep over our nation like a tidal wave.

But now, it's happening again. The blaze of revival fire is cooling down. With the exception of a few hot spots here and there, the Charismatic renewal has become little more than a few smoldering embers. The scandals in the 80's and the imbalances in the faith and prosperity messages that carried us into 21st century has turned what was a mighty healing and soul winning move of God into a selfish "what can I get from God" movement.

What is happening to us? Perhaps it's the same things that caused that early Pentecostal movement to fizzle. *They forgot to remember.* That's right, they forgot to *remember, repent,* and *return.*

> *"Remember the height from which you have fallen!*
> *Repent and do the things you did at first."* — Jesus

Again, things began to fall apart as we allowed worldly attitudes about wealth and self-promotion to infiltrate our ranks. The influx of the "Me Generation" of the late 70's and 80's invaded our churches and knock us off course. The ending results being that too many of our once great soul winning stations have become little more than *bless-me* clubs. The vision for the lost, that once drove us to our knees and then to the streets, faded into visions of financial prosperity. Reconsider these words of the Apostle Paul:

> *If anyone teaches false doctrines and does not agree*
> *to the sound instruction of our Lord Jesus Christ and to*
> *godly teaching, he is conceited and understands nothing.*
> *He has an unhealthy interest in controversies and quarrels*
> *about words that result in envy, strife, malicious talk, evil*
> *suspicions and constant friction between men of corrupt*
> *mind, who have been robbed of the truth and **who think that***
> ***godliness is a means to financial gain.***
> *But godliness with contentment is great gain. For we*
> *brought nothing into the world, and we can take nothing out*

*of it. But if we have food and clothing, we will be content with that. **People who want to get rich fall into temptation and a trap and into many foolish and harmful desires that plunge men into ruin and destruction. For the love of money is a root of all kinds of evil. Some people, eager for money, have wandered from the faith and pierced themselves with many griefs.***

*But you, man of God, **flee from all this [let go of that skirt]**, and pursue righteousness, godliness, faith, love, endurance and gentleness.* (1 Timothy 6:2-11)

Many who once claimed cities for God are now claiming new cars and bank accounts for themselves. Many churches have lost the lamp of revelation and are now stumbling around in darkness and have become little more than scandal centers. Why? We forgot to *remember, repent and return.* God forgive us!

You were running a good race. Who cut in on you and kept you from obeying the truth? (Galatians 5:7)

Charismatic Chaos

Let's be honest shall we? Many of us have fallen victim to some sort of charismatic chaos at one time or other. Many of us have been guilty of doing things like judging a local church's worth by considering how much entertainment value it has. We've determine the value of a church based on how great the worship music is or based on the pastor's pulpit persona, rather than looking at the church's impact on the community and its love for one another.

Many who call themselves "Spirit filled" have abandoned a personal relationship with God and a commitment to a local

body of believers. They started bouncing from place to place
in a relentless search for some mystical thing called, "a word".
These spiritual tumbleweeds have no roots and, therefore, have no
nourishment. Thus, they get caught up in every spiritual fad that
comes along.

> *It was he [Jesus] who gave some to be apostles, some to be*
> *prophets, some to be evangelists, and some to be pastors*
> *and teachers, to prepare God's people for works of service,*
> *so that the body of Christ may be built up until we all reach*
> *unity in the faith and in the knowledge of the Son of God*
> *and **become mature, attaining to the whole measure of the***
> ***fullness of Christ. Then we will no longer be infants, tossed***
> ***back and forth by the waves, and blown here and there by***
> ***every wind of teaching and by the cunning and craftiness***
> ***of men** in their deceitful scheming. Instead, speaking the*
> *truth in love, we will in all things grow up into him who is*
> *the Head, that is, Christ.* (Ephesians 4:11-15)

These *Cruise*-a-matics are a ship without an anchor.
They're tossed from port to port and blown about by every wind
of teaching. Sadly, many have been shipwrecked on the rocks
of fallen spiritual icons and abusive pastors. They have released
their grip on the very foundational principles that birthed the great
Holy Spirit movement in America and have chased after trinkets.
They lost their first love. They have forgotten what those early
pioneers knew—the *why* of the baptism of the Holy Spirit.

"Only the man who lives in fellowship with divine reality can
    be used to call the people to God." — Frank Bartleman [78]

Catch for us the foxes, the little foxes that ruin the vineyards, our vineyards that are in bloom. (Song of Solomon 2:15)

It's time for us to *remember, repent* and *return*. It's imperative that we seek God like never before! We must remember our spiritual roots, the diligence and selflessness that gave birth to this awesome revival. Then we must repent of fleshly attitudes and schemes, those little foxes that were allowed to creep in and ruin our vineyard.

We've got to return to that place where we released our grip on God, latched on to trinkets and lost our direction. If we do this God will meet us there and honor our repentance. He will then pour out his Spirit on us again. Our cup *will* overflow! The results will be glorious! Quite frankly it will be somewhat frightening, as well.

Once we repent and begin to yield to the lordship of Christ, God's glory will once more fill his Church. Then like Isaiah we'll abandon any claim to personal righteousness and begin to submit to his. We'll release our grip on a skirt of religious values and practices which offer only false security. And then, we will latch firmly onto Holy God. Only then will we truly come to know him and the days of *wrong skirt grabbing* will become a thing of the past.

8

THE 'HEAVENLY-MINDED' SKIRT

An Altitude Adjustment

...Letting go of our grip on the sweet bye and bye
and take a long hard look at the dirty here and now?

Let us fix our eyes on Jesus, the author
and perfecter of our faith.

(Hebrews 12:2)

G od did not bring us into the Kingdom of Light in order for us to cower in some bleak bunker and wait for *the second coming.* We weren't endued with the mighty power of the Holy Spirit just for self-preservation. God didn't call us into kingdom service and then leave us dangling, holding on with white knuckles, as we wait for Jesus to return in just the nick of time and rescue us just before our bus plunges into some deep, dark, abyss.

No! No... a thousand times... NO!!! *Since when does darkness overcome light?* When was the last time that you turned on a light switch in a dark room and the light could not shine because the room was just too dark?

Jesus said it clearly. *"YOU are the light of the world. A city on a hill cannot be hidden."*[79] A lamp can light up an entire room. Yet it has no intrinsic light of its own. Its radiance comes from the light that shines within it. The same holds true for you. You have no spiritual light of your own. The source of your light is Jesus. He is the radiance that shines inside of you illuminating those around. It is *his* light within you that overcomes the darkness. "No, in all these things we are more than conquerors *through him* who loved us."[80]

Is Heaven our final destination? No, it's part of God's retirement program for us who gave our lives to him. However, many of us don't see it that way. Instead, we've developed a defeatist attitude that has caused us to look to Heaven more as our deliverer, rather than to Christ. "God is our refuge and strength, an ever-present help in trouble."[81]

In other words, many who profess to know Christ have given up on having any real victory in their personal lives here on

Earth. They've latch onto The Heavenly Minded Skirt. Then they gradually slip into a lethargic, near comatose state, and wait idly for death so that they can go to "a better place." Ultimately what has happened is that they have turned to Heaven as some sort of rescue from the troubles of life rather than turning to Christ for the power to become conquerors over life.

What a sorry crew we've become! It's even reflected in a lot of the Gospel Songs that many of us sing. Instead of Christ -centered anthems of praise and worship, they are Heaven-centered *escapist songs*. They usually carry this sort of theme.

> ♪ Oh, we're all going to Heaven.
> Yes, we're all going to Heaven.
> And the world's going to Hell,
> but we don't give don't care.
> 'cause we're all going to Heaven. ♪

An Altitude Adjustment

> *For those God foreknew he also predestined to be*
> *conformed to the likeness of his Son...*
> (Romans 8:29)

Heaven most certainly awaits the believer at the end of his earthly life. But it's God's retirement plan, not *the* final destination that he has mapped out for us. The word "conformed" in this verse is from a Greek word meaning *to bring to the same form with some person or thing— to render like.* (Wuest) The word "likeness" comes from a Greek word meaning *a derived likeness.* (Wuest) Wuest goes on to say, "The image of the Lord Jesus in the saint is not accidental but derived, as the likeness of a child is derived from its parents."[36] Simply put, *our final destination is to become like Jesus. We're to put on his character and adopt his heart of love and compassion.*

So, if we're to reach this goal we must have, not an attitude adjustment but an *altitude* adjustment. "Since, then, you have been raised with Christ, set your hearts on things above."[82] We need to re-adjust our point of view. We must seriously take a prayerful look at our bus affiliation. Specifically, we need to look at where we are spiritually. We need to consider the attitudes of our fellow passengers and, indeed, look closely at *our* own attitudes. Which means we must also consider where [if anywhere] we are going in our spiritual journey?

Perhaps we need to refine our definition of some of the common terms to which we've grown accustomed; such as Heaven, witnessing, church membership, accountability, and so forth. *Maybe it's time to change buses altogether.* Perhaps we should weigh the possibility that the bus we are currently on will *never* take us to God's final destination for our lives.

The attitude of many believers can be aptly described by the old expression which speaks of those who are "So Heavenly minded that they are of no earthly good." This holds true of many in our western Churches. They have a death-grip on a Heavenly Minded Skirt. However, God is now calling us to embrace a major attitude change! He's saying that it's time to get our heads out of the clouds. In other words, *it's time to get off of that bus!*

Let us fix our eyes on Jesus, the author and perfecter of our faith.
(Hebrews 12:2)

The Greek word used here for "fix" means to take one's gaze off of one thing and then lock it firmly onto another. We *must* be about the Father's business. How do we do this? May I suggest that we start by letting go of our grip on the sweet bye and bye and take a long hard look at the dirty here and now? The world is waiting to see some real love and concern in the lives of today's professing Christians. Yes, Heaven will be a glad reunion day but for the present let's tell some folks how to get there. Shall we? Wait... is that a new bus I hear pulling up?

Religious Wineskins

> *"Remember the height from which you have fallen!*
> *Repent and do the things you did at first.*
> *If you do not repent, I will come to you and*
> *remove your lampstand from its place."*
> — Jesus (Revelation 2:5)

There's a divine summons being presented to the American Church today. God is commanding his people to repent of destructive attitudes that have long plagued us with division and strife. He's demanding that we lay aside fruitless endeavors, renounce self-seeking ways, get back to basics, and then seek a fresh anointing of the Holy Spirit.

I'm not referring to another futile dash of charismatic goose bumps and hysterics that vanish soon after the music dies down. We need a *true* anointing. We need a touch from God that will manifest itself in a Christ-like love and power that simply cannot and *will not* be contained in the same old religious wineskins. Worn out methods and men-centered think-ing will not manifest the character of Jesus. Nor will bull-headed traditionalism or denominational arrogance accommodate what God is about to do in the world. It's time to change buses!

(Some Greeks) came to Philip, who was from Bethsaida
in Galilee, with a request. "Sir," they said,
"we would like to see Jesus."
(John 12:21)

The western Church has been blinded far too long by the *healthy, wealthy and wise* message of the maga-faith/prosperity movement. This sort of distorted teaching has caused those who embrace it to evolve into a self-centered people. They seem bent on seeking only their own comfort while offering little regard for the needs of those around them.

We've ultimately displaced God's focus with that of our own. You see, God's heart has always been on reaching people. He is, therefore, calling us to repent and renounce the selfishness of the past and to get back with the original program—winning the lost to Christ. *It's time we stopped seeking prosperity and started seeking souls. We must divert our attention from our own comfort and look at all the discomfort that surrounds us.* There are millions of hurting, hopeless, dying people who are waiting for us to show them something real or *someone* who is real. Like the Greeks who came to Philip, *they want to see Jesus.*

A seasoned missionary was sent to China many years ago with the commission to translate the Bible into Mandarin Chinese. Upon his arrival he acquired the assistance of a local college student who was alien to the Christian faith but spoke and read fluent English. They then set out to accomplish the monumental task at hand. Weeks soon passed into months as they labored on this all-important project. The missionary was impressed with how tirelessly his youthful co-worker dedicated himself to the tedious task of translating word for word and line upon line of the Bible into his native language. What he did not realize, however, was that he was under close scrutiny as well. For every day that they worked side by side the young Asian carefully noticed everything the missionary did and said. In fact, he in his own way, *was translating the missionary.*

Finally, the big day arrived. Their job was completed. The manuscript was packaged and ready to ship to the Christian publishing house back in America. As they sat drinking tea and celebrating their triumph the missionary spoke.

"Well Lee, now that you've read and studied The Bible from cover to cover what do you think of Christianity?" "I confess, Sir, that I am truly intrigued." he answered. "I am especially impressed with the life of Jesus. In fact, after many weeks of careful consideration, I am very interested in Christianity and would like to become a Christian. Perhaps someday I will meet a Christian and he can tell me how to become one."

The missionary was stunned, uncertain of what he heard. Had his ears betrayed him? "Ah... Lee, I must have misunderstood. You said you would one day like to become a Christian and... "Yes." Lee interrupted. "I hope that one day I will meet a Christian and he will tell me how to become one."

"But... but... *I'm* a Christian, Lee! I *am* a Christian!" the shocked minister returned. Lee was visibly surprised. "*You...* Sir?! *You...* are a Christian? No, that just cannot be, Sir! I have studied the life of Jesus and the lives of early Christians in The Bible. No, no, no, you cannot be a Christian.

"You see Sir, I've watched you closely for these many months now, and I have heard you often complain and get upset at problems we have faced, even though Jesus said, "Let not your heart be troubled." I have even, on occasion, heard you speak ill of those within your organization, as well as saying unkind things about those who are not a part of your church's denomination, even though Jesus said, 'Do not judge or you will be judged.'

"I have seen you filled with anxiety and have observed you pacing back and forth, wringing your hands in worry when money was low and funds from the United States were late in arriving, even though Jesus said... what was it now? Oh yes, 'So do not worry, saying, 'What shall we eat?' or 'What shall we wear?' Your heavenly Father knows that you need them.'

"Also, Sir, and I mean no disrespect, but why in all the months that we have worked together so closely have you never told me of your faith? If you know Jesus, then why have you been silent about him? Why have you not tried to convert me? No, no, *you* are not a Christian! But if I ever meet one, I will ask *him* how I may become a Christian too."

The question that Lee asked the missionary is the one the world is asking the American Church. "Why are you holding back Jesus from us? Why are you so unlike him?" The *Greeks* around us are saying, "We have observed your lives and your churches. Why don't we see Jesus in them? We're not interested in your programs or your buildings or your praise and worship music. We would like to see Jesus! We've seen enough of your hypocrisy, your faithlessness, and lack of peace! You offer nothing more than that which we already have. *We would like to see Jesus!"*

The Coming Storm

See, the storm of the LORD will burst out in wrath,
a whirlwind swirling down on the heads of the wicked.
The anger of the LORD will not turn back until
he fully accomplishes the purposes of his heart.
In days to come you will understand it clearly.
(Jeremiah 23:19-20)

"God who gave us life gave us liberty. And can the liberties of a nation be thought secure when we have removed their only firm basis, a conviction in the minds of the people that these liberties are a gift from God? That they are not to be violated but with His wrath? Indeed I tremble for my country when I reflect that God is just, and that His justice cannot sleep forever." (These words are inscribed on the walls of the Jefferson Memorial in our nation's capital)[83]

I believe that God is about to transform the marred image of the American church. The wheels of judgment are beginning to turn. Purging is on its way. Like the rumble of distant thunder announces a coming storm, current events in Washington D.C. and across this nation are proclaiming the depth of our national sin sickness, and the judgment it is bringing on us. I sense that we have finally forced God's hand. I fear that America has gone too far! *God must now act!*

Righteousness exalts a nation,
but sin is a disgrace to any people.
(Proverbs14:34)

What has happened to this country who once proclaimed herself to be "One nation under God?" In 1776 we declared our independence from Great Britain. We were a people who honored God. He reciprocated by making America strong and blessing us over-abundantly. In time we became the greatest nation on Earth. The Lord continued to bless us as long as we acknowledged ourselves a nation whose dependence was on him.

Then in 1962 we made another declaration of independence when we declared our independence from God. And since that terrible day when the Supreme Court announced that God is not welcome in our public schools anymore,[84] America has slipped deeper and deeper into rebellion and moral decay. And the trend continues today as many of our nation's leaders have persistently snubbed their noses at God and his commands.

"I will take vengeance in anger and wrath upon
the nations that have not obeyed me."
(Micah 5:15)

"If God doesn't judge America he will have to resurrect Sodom and Gomorrah and apologize to them!"[85]

For we know him who said, "It is mine to avenge;
I will repay," and again, "The Lord will judge his people."
It is a dreadful thing to fall into the hands of the living God."
(Hebrews 10:30-31)

Again I say I feel that we have crossed over a line that leaves God with no other alternative but to release his judgment. God is preparing the crucible, the anvil, and the hammer. I believe that a purifying fire of intense heat, such as we have never seen, is about to sweep across this nation.

A Purpose behind the Purging

However, don't lose hope as you see these things
unfolding, my friend. Look up for that which is coming is not all
doom and gloom. There is a purpose behind the purging. I believe
that what is about to come is necessary in order to prepare us to
receive an unparalleled end time harvest.

> *"And no one pours new wine into old wineskins.*
> *If he does, the new wine will burst the skins,*
> *the wine will run out and the wineskins will be ruined.*
> *No, new wine must be poured into new wineskins."*
> — Jesus (Luke 5:37-38)

The American church in its present condition cannot
contain what God is about to pour out on her. She has too many
old wineskins. In other words, she is so heavy laden with dead,
old, stale religious attitudes that she can't possibly hold a fresh
move of God. The American church cannot at present stand under
an outpouring so powerful that it will shake this nation to its very
foundation. She must first, once for all, repent and renounce skirt
grabbing. In other words, she must cast aside those old religious
wineskins. Man-made institutions and worn out, antiquated
attitudes can't possibly hold a tumult of this magnitude.

> *"But He knows the way that I take; when He*
> *has tested me, I will come forth as gold."*
> (Job 23:10)

Yes, God is once again about to pour out his Spirit on all
flesh, but first he must prepare us to receive it. Therefore, it is
essential that we repent and be ready to empty ourselves of any

and all hindrances that would block that which God desires to do in us! God cannot fill a vessel that is already full of other things, such as fixations that are alien to his purposes. Nor will he pour his anointing into a container that is filthy.

Would you pour milk into a dirty glass that you just picked up out of a city dumpster and then offer it to your child? Of course not! Neither will God. He refuses to place the milk of his Word into filthy vessels and then offer it to a hungry world! We've got to clean up our act! We must first repent and rid ourselves of nasty attitudes or any sinful behavior that would block the outpouring that is to come. *We must be willing to make room for what God wants to do in us. If not, he will find someone who is willing. It's just that simple.*

Gold in poetic scripture, such as Job, is symbolic of the righteousness of God. The word "testing" that Job speaks of is from a root Hebrew word that refers to the purification of metals. God *will* purify the attitudes and conduct of his church. The world *will* again see an outward expression of the righteousness of God in the Church. They *will* see Jesus! That is once the old wineskins and wrong skirt grabbing are done away with. God desires for you to be a part of what he's about to do. Please pay heed to my words, my friend, lest you miss it!

The Sound of the Trumpet

The days of punishment are coming, the days of reckoning are at hand. Let [the U.S.A] know this. Because your sins are so many and your hostility so great, the prophet is considered a fool, the inspired man a maniac.

(Hosea 9:7)

Oh, my anguish, my anguish! I writhe in pain.
Oh, the agony of my heart!
My heart pounds within me, I cannot keep silent.
For I have heard the sound of the trumpet;
I have heard the battle cry.
(Jeremiah 4:19)

I know that what I'm saying may sound foolish to some and perhaps to others the ravings of a maniac bent on frightening people. However, if I am labeled so then at least I find myself in very good company. I have consulted several who are tuned in to what the Spirit is saying to the churches. I have talked with Pastors and other great men and women of God. Many are declaring the same warning. God's watchmen are sounding the alarm. They are blowing trumpets of warning all over this nation. Indeed, the Churches in our nation had better wake up and smell the proverbial coffee!

Please believe me when I say that my intentions are honorable before God. He will judge my heart and call me to account if my motives are amiss. You don't know how much I want to be wrong about the impending fire that I see. Please join me as I pray for our nation that God will extend his mercy to her. Repent with me as I repent for the sins of the American church. We have lost our saltiness, our influence, in the land. Let us pray that it is not too late to regain that which we have lost. Perhaps if we do, God will stay his hand of judgment.

I fear, however, that it may be too late for that. The horse is already out of the barn. It's too late to shut the door. The trumpet of judgment is sounding a clear warning. When I watch the news I hear its blast echoing from sea to shining sea, and I suspect that it is on its way. Indeed it may already have arrived. I pray it has not.

However, take heart my friend. God is about to do an awesome work, but he needs us to be ready for it. I want to be prepared for the glory that will follow. Don't you? Don't you want to partake in possibly the greatest revival this nation has ever seen? First comes the purging as the Holy Spirit beckons us to repent of all our skirt grabbing, then comes revival! It's always been that way. Are you ready to board *that* bus my friend? Be assured that it's on its way. If you listen very closely you will hear the roar of its mighty engine just over the horizon.

Twilight Zone Saints

Forgetting what is behind and straining toward what is ahead,
*I press on toward the goal **to win the prize** for which God*
has called me heavenward in Christ Jesus.
(Philippians 3:13-14)

Many Christians will never find God's bus. They will never arrive at their final destination. They've found their comfort zone and are not willing to change buses. The reason for their hesitation may be that they're fearful, spiritually ignorant, or just plain willful. They miss out on what God wants to do in their lives. They boarded a particular spiritual bus that goes a certain distance and no further, but they refuse to change buses.

As stated earlier, change *is* frightening! Therefore, this contented congregation remains right where they are. The bus these spiritual squatters are on, may leave them completely unsatisfied or even downright miserable at times. Nevertheless, it's a bus that was passed down to them from generation to generation. It's a bus that they've been on all their lives and to which they have grown accustomed. Their bus may not take them anywhere new and exciting but at least it's safe. It's undemanding, uneventful, but also devoid of any real satisfaction or power.

Sadly they will remain on their bus of choice, or in that movement or denomination, with others who also refuse to leave. There they ride, doomed to travel around in circles like characters in some bizarre Twilight Zone episode. Thus, they will never arrive at that crucial *final destination*. They will eventually die and stand before God having never known his best for their lives, just like their fathers did and their father's fathers did before. Oh yes! *Give me that old time religion... It's good enough for me.*[86]

Frozen Motion

It's a traditional mind-set, a comfort zone that was passed down from generation to generation. You know, sort of like a pew. Just go into your basic local church some Sunday morning and try to sit on someone's pew. Just try it. I *dare* you! You'll quickly find that church members are as territorial as bears when it comes to their pews.

"What are you doing on my pew, boy?! That's *my* pew! It was my Pappy's pew before me, and before that it was my Grand-pappy's pew. As a matter of fact, my Great-grand-pappy had a chair that set right there on that very spot before this church was built. It was passed all the way down to me and I intend to sit there if I have to sit in your lap! Now, *move it or lose it!* Why don't you set on one of them front pews. They're most *always* empty anyway."

These *Zonies* become yet another victim of The Wrong Skirt Effect. Their battle cry is "The Seven Words of Death". "That's not the way I was taught!" or "We have always done it that way!" They have, of their own accord, adopted a sanctimonious lifestyle that leaves them trapped on the same old bus, forever imprisoned in a religious rut.

> Definition of a rut: *a grave with the ends kicked out.*
> —unknown

> ... *having a form of godliness but denying its power.*
> (2 Timothy 3:5)

The Greek word for *form* here means *a form or an outline.* In the New Testament, it denotes an *outward semblance.*[87] In essence, these stifled saints have become locked into a deadly pattern of the commonplace. It looks right because it's that for which they're accustomed. It has an outward *semblance* of the truth, but is it the truth? Or is it just another wrong skirt?

Treasury agents can easily pick out a bogus bill that was made by the cleverest counterfeiter. Why? They're able to pick out a phony because they have studied the *real* thing thoroughly. What these *Zonies*[88] have looks real to them simply because they haven't had much of the bona fide article with which to compare it. They've allowed this pseudo-religion to dull their inner spiritual longing. It does this by offering a *form,* or semblance, of godliness— *a counterfeit*. But like all counterfeits, it's completely worthless. It is, therefore, dead and devoid of true power.

Yet these Zonies seem content to cruise along on their familiar old bus unable, or perhaps *unwilling,* to break free of its entrapment. What a shame! For they are ultimately condemned to a life of traveling around in circles and clinging to a cheap imitation of the real thing. Blindly contented, they continue to ride the same old go-no-where bus, stuck in a frozen motion with the same old go-no-where people. Forever trapped in a spiritual *Twilight Zone*, they are unable to experience the life changing power of a true encounter with our awesome God

The Devil's Merry-go-round

What a waste of gifts and talents! How heart rending it is when people with so much potential for The Kingdom of God, just lay aside any possibilities outside the commonplace. *How it must grieve God's heart to watch his children commit themselves to a system of religious and traditional practices that represses growth and then for them to spend their energies becoming conformed to it rather than to Christ!*

A policeman happened upon a car in an empty parking lot. The driver was just driving around in circles as fast as his car would go. After observing this strange scene for about 20 minutes he turned on his siren and flashing lights. The man saw the police car and brought his car to a screeching halt.

The policeman, with ticket pad in hand, walked over to the car. "License and registration, please." He said as he peered into the driver's open window. "Why were you driving around in circles. Are you lost? Where are you heading?" "Nowhere, officer," said the driver. "… but I'm making good time."

These Zonies are confined in a self-imposed prison and

are slated to ride the Devil's Merry-go-round going nowhere. They spin around and around in a vicious cycle. Their Christianity is spent doing and saying the same old useless things, thinking all the while that since they're seeing movement they must be making progress. Yet the harsh reality is that they are only going in circles and are destined to never arrive at God's best for them.

They follow the example of the Children of Israel who were condemned to wander around in a wasteland for forty years.[89] Why? They resisted change. They had been on an Egyptian bus for 400 years and were reluctant to get off. Sure, it was a painful ordeal being under the heavy hand of their taskmasters, but they had grown accustomed to it. *They had found their comfort zone and were afraid to go on with God.*

This has got to be the greatest disaster that can befall a child of God. So many professing Christians are like those Israelites. They are unwilling to do something radical to change their circumstances. The Israelites refused to obey God because of their fear of the unknown. They chose to believe men rather than believing God. They would rather continue their go-nowhere cycle in the wilderness than to receive God's best.

If you want God to do so something radical in your life, you must be willing to do something radical!

Like the Israelites many of today's professing Christians are paralyzed by some hand-me-down religious mindset that keeps them roaming around in a spiritual wilderness. They are glued to the devil's merry-go-round. If they don't do something of a radical nature they will be robbed of the unspeakable joy that comes only from serving and knowing God. They will remain bound in the chains of human traditions that demand that they know church covenants and practices at the expense of knowing God.

> "You cannot stay where you are and go on with God."
> - Henry T. Blackaby [90]

Swinging on a Star

> "Insanity: doing the same thing over and
> over again and expecting different results."
> - Albert Einstein[91]

May I ask you a question? What skirt are you holding on to? Do you have a firm hold on truth at any cost, even at the cost of your denominational upbringing? Or do you have a death grip on the familiar, the comfortable, and the uneventful? Are you happy with low living? Or would you like to swing on a star? In other words, is God birthing something inside you that cries out to be released? Is there a greatness stirring within your breast but fear of change causes you to suppress it?

Are you stuck on the devil's merry-go-round? Are you fastened into a fixed pattern of attending go-no-where churches where, Sunday after Sunday, year end and year out, the same old people do the same old things and have very little, if any, impact on their community. Or worst yet, do you feel no significant stirring within at all and you're perfectly satisfied with your life where it is right now?

If your answer is "yes" to this last question, may I make a strong recommendation? Will you please consider the possibility that you have never truly surrendered your life to Christ! I'm not talking about a *shake-hands-with-the-preacher-my-names-on-the-*

roll-salvation. NO! You need a *saved-to-the-bone-Jesus-is-Lord-and-I'm-sold-out-to-the-max-salvation!* Which when you get right down to it, is really the only kind that God offers.

The Stirring

*As the time approached for him to be taken up to heaven, Jesus resolutely set out for Jerusalem. And he sent messengers on ahead, who went into a Samaritan village to get things ready for him; **but the people there did not welcome him, because he was heading for Jerusalem.***
(Luke 9:51-53)

Perhaps you're sure of your salvation and that God will welcome you into Heaven. Yet, you realize that you are caught in a deadly cycle of stale religious rhetoric and you don't quite know how to be free? The thought of change frightens you, but you desperately want to be free to respond to that urging from God that wells up within you..

If this is you, you're not alone. So many professing Christians are like that. They go through life seemingly satisfied with living at a certain spiritual summit, suppressing the occasional stirring that they feel. Many seldom consider change and feel threatened by those who go beyond established limits. Too often in an effort to excuse their own willful disobedience, they do as their religious forerunners have done. They criticize and act suspiciously toward those who push the envelope and press on beyond the norm.

So if you make that decision to press on by obeying God, be prepared. For soon you will find that the Samaritans, whom you once rode around in circles with, will now offer to you a

cold shoulder instead of a warm embrace. In the same way that
the Samaritans refused to welcome Jesus because they didn't
like where he was going, your fellow passengers will refuse your
fellowship because of where you are going. The reason for their
disapproval is simple; you made them feel uncomfortable. I know
from personal experience that this is true.

So the chief priests made plans to kill Lazarus as well, for on
account of him many of the Jews were going over to Jesus and
putting their faith in him. (John 12:10-11)

As Jesus commanded Lazarus[92] to come out of his grave,
he is calling you to come out your grave of religious bondage
and live. Just don't be surprised when self-righteous members of
your church, or denomination, try to kill you. They may not take
your physical life, but they will try to destroy your reputation as a
Christian. Devout Christian friends and even family members will
talk shamelessly about you behind your back. They will denounce
your bus. They will try to discredit your relationship with the
Lord in order that they may feel better about their bus.

Sadly, multitudes of believers refuse to change buses at
the next terminal, and get with the program. They set on their
bus and judge everyone who gets off and changes buses. Yet,
God continues to call them to come and be free from that deadly
cadence that leads to nowhere. Like the Israelites of old they
remain unmoved by his plea and continue wondering around in
the wilderness.

If this sounds dangerously close to where you are
spiritually and you've settled the issue of your salvation, then

I have another recommendation. Meet with God and do a thorough evaluation of your bus affiliation. Prayerfully go over the questionnaire in chapter four and see if your heart is in sync with that of your church or denomination. If you have been truly honest with God and with yourself, then the chances are you will discover that you are caught in a dead-end pattern—a comfort zone—and your life is being wasted on aimless pursuits.

Further Instructions

You may be thinking to yourself, "That sure sounds like me. I think I might be trapped in my own comfort zone, clinging to the wrong skirt, but how do I find out for certain? Are there any other practical steps that I can take that will give me some needed answers?" Yes there are, and they're really quite simple.

First, begin with prayer. Ask the Holy Spirit to open your spiritual eyes and show you the truth no matter how unpleasant it may seem to you at the time. Next, take the authority which has been delegated to you by the Lord Jesus[93] and bind the mouth of the demonic forces from interfering.

Now, you're ready to give yourself a short pop quiz. Start by prayerfully considering this question. "Where was I in my spiritual journey a year ago, two years ago, or even five years ago?" Then ask yourself, "Am I still in the same place spiritually? Am I right where I've always been?" Then ask yourself, "Has there been any detectable change in me or my situation? Am I really going anywhere? And if so, where am I going?"

Too much is at stake, my friend. It is imperative that you be painfully honest as you ask yourself this final question. "Can I hope to see any noticeable progress in my walk with the Lord a

year from now, that is if I remain on the bus I am on right now?'
Note: A good way to gauge the prospect of any future progress is
to look at your fellow passengers (church members)—those who
have been on your bus for 20, 30, 40 years. Guess what? *That's
the future you!*

Now having completed your assignment let's cut to the
chase. If you have been honest with God and have discovered that
your spiritual condition remains unaltered year after year, after
year, after *boring* year, then as you look ahead you see no reversal
in your condition coming in the near future. Then may I ask one
final question? In light of this new found revelation, do you still
refuse change?! If so, then in the name of God, WHY!

> *You were running a good race. Who cut in on*
> *you and kept you from obeying the truth?*
> (Galatians 5:7)

The Price of Revelation

> *Do not merely listen to the word, and so deceive yourselves.*
> ***Do what it says.*** *Anyone who listens to the word but does*
> *not do what it says is like a man who looks at his face*
> *in a mirror and, after looking at himself, goes away and*
> *immediately forgets what he looks like. But the man who*
> *looks intently into the perfect law that gives freedom, and*
> *continues to do this,* ***not forgetting what he has heard, but***
> ***doing it*** *– he will be blessed in what he does.*
> (James 1:22-25)

> *Then the LORD said,*
> *"My Spirit will not contend with man forever…"*
> (Genesis 6:3a)

Revelation demands obedience! Obedience is manifested in change and a closer walk with God. Suppose I get up in the morning and look at myself in the bathroom mirror. (I know it's a revolting thought but work with me.) I'm shocked beyond measure! I rub my eyes and look again. "Oh, man! My hair looks like it came in for a crash landing on my head! My face looks like it was sponged off with a porcupine and my breath smells like a wino's armpit!" I then take a close look at my clothes. "*Yech!* Look at the big ink stain on my shirt! And my tie, someone must have used it to wipe off the kitchen table. WHAT A SLOB!! I need to make some changes before I go out." I hurry out of the bathroom, leaping over a mountainous pile of dirty clothes and rush into the kitchen to get a coffee refill. As I'm dipping my second scoop of creamer, I notice the clock on the oven. "Ahhhhh!! Look at the time!"

I grab my coat and charge out the kitchen door, tripping over the trash can in the garage. It's contents spill everywhere! My foot slips on some old banana peels and my cup of steaming hot coffee flies out of my hand. The cup then does a beautiful two and a half gainer and lands squarely on the hood of my car, scalding the neighbor's cat! "Weeoul!!!" "Serves you right for sleeping on my stinking car!" I fumble around in my trouser pockets for my car keys and opened the door. I then slide behind the wheel. Before you can say Richard Petty, I'm racing down the road.

What has happened? (Other than the fact that the neighbor's cat has learned a valuable lesson about respecting other people's property) You guessed it! I forgot how I looked. The mirror gave me clear revelation about my appearance. How did I respond? I did not heed the mirrors solid warning that some changes needed to be made about my appearance.

If you had responded to my rebuke, I would have poured out my heart to you and made my thoughts known to you.
(Proverbs 1:23)

Again, the price of revelation is obedience! Obedience is manifested in change. When you look "intently" into the Word of God, it's like looking at yourself in a spiritual mirror. Specific areas in your life that need change are uncovered. Wrong skirts that you didn't even know you were clinging to will be exposed. However, if you do not respond in obedience by modifying your behavior, God will shut down communications. He will not make his thoughts known to you. The heavens will become brass and you will not hear so much as a whisper of revelation from him.

"God doesn't just tell you things for information
but for transformation."
— Henry T. Blackaby[94]

An old Chinese proverb says, "A journey of a thousand miles begins with but one step." Becoming like Christ is a step by step, revelation to revelation, change by change, bus to bus process. Obedience is essential! If you're not willing to take that next step and obey the current revelation that God has given you about your life's direction, he will not give you fresh revelation about future steps.

Step by Step

Your word is a lamp to my feet and a light for my path.
(Psalms 119:105)

If you've ever walked down an unfamiliar wooded path
in the dead of night with only a kerosene lamp to light the way,
then you have a clear picture of what David was trying to say.
The lamps that were used in his day were not very bright. They
consisted of a small container of oil that had a single flame. This
flame was bright enough to light one's path only about a step at a
time. A traveler could not see beyond a single step and, therefore,
could not safely proceed beyond the illuminated area around
his feet. He would have to take a step before the next step was
illuminated. Then he would take another step into the illumination
then another step and so forth.

Unfortunately, Zonies will not take the next step. I can see
it now. Here's some poor traveler with only a single small flame
to light his way in the night. He looks ahead and sees nothing but
darkness. "Oooo, that's scary!" he says to himself. "I don't know
what's out there!" He lowers his gaze to the small circle of light
at his feet. "Ah... now, that's more like it! I think I'll hang around
here where there's some light."

Hang around he does... and around, and around, and
around, and... Well, you get the idea. Sadly, he has doomed
himself to going around in circles and remaining in the limited
light that he has when there is so much more of the path ahead
waiting to be discovered. Eventually his lamp begins to run out of
oil. He stares in horror at the flickering flame as the gloom closes
in around him. There's little more than fumes left, now, and the
only thing awaiting him is total darkness.

Many believers have a well worn path encircling their
feet. This path constitutes their comfort zone. They resist change
with every ounce of their strength and then wonder why they

cannot hear God. I repeat; the price of revelation is obedience! Obedience is manifested in change. If you're not willing to respond to God's revelation by proceeding to the next terminal and then changing buses, he will remain silent. Your growth will be stifled. What you do will not be blessed. You'll sit idly by and watch others walk on in the power and the light of the Holy Spirit. Furthermore, the place where you are right now in your life *will be* your final destination!

9

THE END OF SKIRT-GRABBING

Don't Try To Fix What
God is Trying to Break

W e just can't trust someone we don't know.

Jesus answered, "I am the way and the truth and the life."

(John14:6)

W hy do so many professing Christians have a death grip on wrong skirts like those described in the preceding chapters? Exactly where did they miss it? Why do they not realize that what they are clinging to is the wrong skirt? The reason is elementary. They don't recognize the truth, because they don't *know* the truth. Why don't they know the truth? *Because they don't really know Jesus!*

Oh they know their particular choice of skirt well enough. Many have made life studies of skirt-grabbing. They just don't recognize the one who said, "I am the truth." Therefore, it becomes a simple case of mistaken identity that leads them into various types of deception. They latch onto imitations of the truth and continue wasting their lives away—victims of The Wrong Skirt Effect.

Why is it that so many professing Christians do not know God? The answer to that question is plain to see; they are not willing to *pay* for the privilege. *There is a price involved in getting to know God. This is the key to obtaining power, overwhelming victory and a deeper revelation of God's Word. If you don't get anything else from this book, you must get this!* Understanding this truth is paramount if you wish to once and for all put an end to distractions, religious or otherwise, that would cause you to latch onto the counterfeit and thus miss God's direction!

> *"...any of you who does not give up everything*
> *he has cannot be my disciple."* — Jesus
> (Luke 14:33)

The Price of Wisdom

A young man, eager for the things that make men great, went to seek the advice of a renowned sage. He packed his few meager belongings and began his journey from his home in the valley to the top of the mountain where the legendary master lived. The long journey took him up mountain paths and through treacherous terrain until, alas, he arrived at his destination.

The directions he received from those he encountered along the way led him to an ancient cottage with a tattered roof surrounded by pines and nestled at the end of a twisted path. As he approached the stone structure his heart began to race. His weariness began to subside. A lone figure was sitting... no, he was kneeling in front of the cottage. The traveler quietly drew nearer. And as he approached, he beheld an old man kneeling on a colorful but tattered rug.

"This must be the one that I have sought for so long." he thought. There was no mistaking the description that was given him. "You will find an old man, as ancient as the mountain, living in a stone cottage surrounded by a grove of thick pines. Just follow this path. It will lead you there." Yes, this *was* he.

The young seeker stood silently and reverently. He studied the old man, who was kneeling with face to the ground. A faded robe covered all but his bare, dusty feet. His discarded sandals lay neatly to the side near a knotted cane. The lad listened but heard only the low murmuring of a man paying homage to his God.

The praying ceased and he raised his face to the heavens. A crown of silver caressed a leathered face that bore the evidence of the many years it had witnessed. A crystal tear coursed down his wrinkled cheek and disappeared into a forest of gray. Afraid to speak, the youth could only remain still, dumbfounded and humbled by this picture of greatness bowing in the presence of *He* who is greater.

Finally, the silence was broken. "How can an old man be of service to one so young?" He somehow knew that the boy was there even though his eyes remained closed. "I... ah... Sir, I have come from a long distance... to... ah... " His voice began to tremble as he realized that he was something of an intruder on this private moment.

"Come, come my son. You have nothing to fear from an old man." His voice was gentle and beckoning. "What can I do for you?" As he spoke he reached for his cane and raised himself to his feet. "Walk with me." he said. He slipped his feet into his sandals and began walking away without waiting for a response. The boy finally broke free of his stupor and hurried to catch up.

They walked through the pines with neither man speaking for what seemed an eternity. At last, the old man's ancient voice broke the silence. "So... you seek wisdom?" It was more of a pronouncement than a question. The youth froze in his tracks. "How did you...?" "How badly do you desire it?" he continued, ignoring the boy's bewilderment. "Ah... greatly, Sir! I want it more than life!"

The youth's desire overcame his intimidation. "I would give all that I have, Master. I would sacrifice anything." "Would you, young man... really sacrifice *anything*?!" With that the old one suddenly turned, startling his visitor. "*Anything?*" he demanded. After a moment of stunned silence the lad swallowed then answered. "Yes... Yes, I would... anything! *Anything!* Please tell me. How may I obtain wisdom?"

"Come with me." the sage said and then abruptly turned back toward the cottage. The youth followed, amazed at the quick pace of one so old. They soon arrived at the site of a large metallic basin setting on the round surface of a stone table, which was roughly the circumference of a cart wheel. As they drew nearer the boy saw that it was filled with water. The sage walked to the side of the table and, with a wave, beckoning the boy to join him.

The boy was puzzled but remained determined. He cautiously moved alongside the old man. "So young man, you desire wisdom more than life itself, do you?" he said peering deeply into the boy's eyes. "Yes... ah, yes Master, I do."

Suddenly with the swiftness of a striking cobra the old man grasped the back of the youth's neck in a vice-like grip. In the next instant the sage plunged the boy's face well below the surface of the water!

The surprise was complete. Confusion and panic rushed through the lad's mind as he waved his arms wildly about. He tried with all his strength to break free of the old man's powerful clasp but could not. The greater he struggled the more his attacker held him fast.

Finally, with his strength spent and his lungs ready to explode, he realized the inevitable. He was about to die. This was what his long, arduous quest had brought him—murdered in his youth by some crazed old man. Darkness began closing around him and he felt himself began to drift away.

Then, just as suddenly, he felt himself being yanked from the watery darkness! A long gasp... then air, *wonderful* air, rushed into his lungs! Blinding sunshine greeted his eyes! He threw his arms up to block the painful glare. His senses returned and he felt a tug on the back of his shirt. It was the old man holding him up by a handful of fabric. The boy quickly shoved him away and pulled free.

"ARE YOU MAD!" he screamed, the panic still fresh. "You tried to drown me... WHY?!" The sage reached out to him. "NO! Stay away from me!" He swept his long wet hair from his eyes and continued in short painful breaths. "Don't... (Gasp!)... Don't... come near me! Do you hear?! Keep away!!"

The old man stepped back slightly and stood with both hands resting on his cane. "You said you wanted wisdom, did you not?" he said calmly.

"Yes, but... you tried to..."

"SILENCE!" There was no anger in the sage's voice but only authority — the authority of a man who was used to being hearkened to. "Did you not ask me to teach you how to obtain wisdom? Answer me or be gone with you!" he demanded.

"Yes... yes, but... but why? I don't understand... why..."

The eyes of the old man softened as he continued in low, quieting tones. "Listen my son, and mark well the lesson you learned in the water basin this day. For you will *only* obtain wisdom when you desire it more than you craved that next breath of air. When you want it more than life, more than breath itself; when you are willing to give everything you have, then, and *only* then, will you have it." With that the old one turned, and without another word, disappeared into the darkened doorway of his small cottage.

The Moses Deficit

Wisdom is supreme; therefore get wisdom.
Though it cost all you have, get understanding. (Proverbs 4:7)

When The Proverbs speak of wisdom, it is most always a reference to knowing God and his ways. In fact, the knowledge of God and wisdom are generally synonymous in scripture. *To seek wisdom is to seek God.*

Are you ready to go on with God? Are you weary of the mundane? How sick of skirt grabbing are you? How badly do you want to know truth—*to know God?* How earnestly do you crave wisdom? The scope of your effort will determine the intensity of your desire. Do you truly ache for his presence? If so, are you willing to discard all the skirts of the past and go for God? What price are you willing to pay for the wonderful joy of knowing our Lord? I mean... *for real!*

"Mediocrity is the greatest insult. It says, 'God, I know you. It just doesn't excite me.'" — Dr. Adrian Rogers[95]

To know God is the highest calling there is! Yet, the major bulk of the body of Christ settles for only a superficial knowledge of God. Oh, they feel like they know God or may even profess to know him. They just act like they're not overly excited about it. May I ask you a personal question? Are you an Israelite or a Moses?

One of my closest and dearest long time friends is Bob Lubell, president of Partners for Christian Media in Chattanooga, Tennessee. Some years ago Bob and I were traveling across Tennessee, skipping from town to town, making business calls back when Bob sold fire extinguishers. We we're cruising along a secluded highway, chatting about whatever came to mind and enjoying the plush green scenery for which "The Volunteer State" is famous. I was taking a breath and giving Bob a chance to air his views. We were very close to solving all the world's woes including poverty, world hunger, and Bob was just about to offer a cure for cancer when suddenly I interrupted.

"McNairy County?!"

"What?" he responded.

"Why... it's McNairy County!" I squealed bouncing up and down on my seat like a child silently announcing, "I gotta wee-wee... NOW!" "It's McNairy County Bob!" I was beside myself.

"Yeah... so?" he responded. By now he was wondering if I had finally lost it, and perhaps he should leap from the speeding car and scurry for cover before I started salivating and growing hair on my nose.

"Come on Bob! *You* know... Buford Pusser!"[96] My voice was getting very close to that pitch that only dogs can hear.

"Who?" he asked. He began to calm down once he noticed that there was no full moon.

"You know... *Walking Tall.* The movie... Buford!"

"Ah... no, never heard of him." he returned.

"Are you serious?!!" I shot back. "He's just the most celebrated Lawman since Wyatt Earp! They made three movies about him and even had a T.V. series. He's probably the most famous Tennessean since Davy Crockett!" His curiosity was primed by now, and I had his full attention.

"Let's stop for awhile, O.K.?" I pleaded.

Bob listened as I unfolded the extraordinary true saga of this six foot six, two hundred-fifty pound former pro-wrestler who alone, with a hand full of loyal deputies, stood against organized crime along the Tennessee-Mississippi border. I told of how his weapon of choice was not a .357 magnum, but a long club carved from a tree limb.

Several attempts were made on Buford's life. He was shot eight times and stabbed seven. On one occasion, he was gunned down by some unknown assailant and left for dead on a dark secluded highway. Then there was the terrible day that he was horribly disfigured, and the life of his beloved wife was snuffed out in a cowardly ambush. This remarkable man survived attempt after attempt upon his life, only to ironically lose it in a blazing car crash long after he left office. Bob was aptly impressed and soon became excited about stopping, as well.

We continued only a short distance before spotting a small green sign announcing that we were entering the town of Selmer, Tennessee, which is where the county seat is located. A much larger one posted just beyond the smaller sign offered the friendly greeting, "The Churches of Selmer Welcome You!" We soon found ourselves traveling down narrow streets that were overshadowed with ancient oaks. They seemed to be holding hands as they spread their leafy arms toward one another creating a green canopy that shaded entire streets. "Let's find the courthouse." I suggested. "Maybe we can get some information about Buford there."

No sooner had I spoken than the trees opened, and there it was. The antiquated structure was typical of many small southern county seats which housed both the courtroom and the sheriff's office. More trees like those which graced the streets of Selmer surrounded the ivy covered building. Locals sat lazily on shaded rod-iron benches while indulging in polite chit-chat about the

weather and current events. Large white pillars, glistening in
the noon day sun, lined the front of the courthouse lending that
certain aristocratic, old south appearance.

We drove around to the back of the structure where
the county jail was located. The parking lot was cluttered with
cars. Many had the familiar blue and red lights on top with the
McNairy County Sheriff logo printed on the front doors. The
place was a hive of activity. Cars and pick-up trucks were going
in and out. Two bright natured good-ole-boys were waving and
shouting out cheery greetings as they slowly passed each other.
"How y-all a-doing there, Bill?" "Oh... can't complain Fred.
How's about y-self?" "Well, I was better, but I got over it!" With
that they both gave huge belly laughs (as if they had never heard
that line before), and with the toss of a hand they were gone.

Bob was wheeling his VW Jetta into the parking lot
hoping to find a vacancy, when we spotted two men standing
together and talking. They seemed oblivious to all the hubbub
surrounding them. "Let's ask them." I said and rolled down my
window. The hot, humid, air rushed in to greet us as I poked my
face out of the window.

"Hello!" I shouted. They turned their heads to see who the
loony was hollering at them across the busy parking lot. I must
have put them in mind of an old hound hanging his head out of
his master's car window and barking just for the sake of barking.
The older of the two smiled and nodded a polite greeting, but the
younger turned and approached our car.

"May I help you?" he asked. He was a smartly dressed,
modish looking man of about thirty-five. He appeared to be
somewhat out of place amidst the cover-all set. A shinny

badge flashed in the sunlight from where it hung on his belt, and I thought of the old puzzles that sometimes still appear in magazines.

They would show something like a beautiful sun drenched beach. However, there were things in the picture that did not belong, such as a penguin spread out on a beach blanket. The caption read, "What is wrong with this picture?" I was impressed with the fact that this man did not look like he belonged in this picture. The other people passing back and forth fit right into this classic small southern town setting, but he looked more like he just stepped off of the cover of *G.Q. Magazine*.

"Yes." I answered. "We're from over in the Chattanooga area and we're just passing through and thought we'd stop and ask about Buford." That caused an enormous smile to spread across his face. "Oh... Okay." he said. "I'm the sheriff here. We're glad you're here!" He was positively beaming. "Why don't you go to Buford's house in Adamsville. His mother lives there. Mrs. Pusser loves to have company and loves to talk about her son." With that he proceeded to give us precise directions, and we soon found ourselves setting in the dining room of the most famous lawman since Elliot Ness.

Mrs. Pusser sat across from us at a large oblong dark mahogany table that was covered with opened family albums. She pointed at pictures of aunts, uncles, and cousins and joyously talked about her famous son. The dining room adjoined a huge living room that could have qualified for a Buford Pusser museum [Since the death of Mrs. Pusser in 1987 the house has become the official Buford Pusser Museum]. The walls were literally covered with memorabilia. The traditional photos and family portraits were surrounded by framed newspaper articles, pictures of Buford standing with famous people as well as movie posters from the films based on his life. It was a real treat for a history and movie buff like me. I'll never forget the day I got to go to Buford Pusser's house, and I'll always remember meeting that gracious little lady.

He made known His ways to Moses,
His deeds to the people of Israel
(Psalm 103:7)

Looking back on that experience, I'm reminded of these words of the Psalmist. Let me paraphrase. "Israel only knew *about* God. Moses actually *knew* God!" The Hebrew word used here for *ways* is *derek*. This is literally translated "a road (as trodden)" or figuratively, "a course of life or mode of action."[97]

I knew about the deeds of Mrs. Pusser's famous son. I saw the movies. I read about his life and exploits, but she personally *knew Buford's ways*. She personally knew his *course of life*, his *mode of action*. She knew what made him tick. She knew his heart in a way I never would, because *she personally knew him*. I, on the other hand, only knew about him. Furthermore, she was excited about knowing her son and would freely tell anyone who would listen about him.

There is a real Moses deficit in the western church. You see, you have your Israelites (the skirt grabbers), and then you have your Moses' (the God seekers). At best, Israelites are content with only a superficial relationship with God. They proceed to a certain point where their *Christian walk* turns into a *sit in*. They've found their comfort zone. They've got a strong hold on their favorite skirt and that's where they'll stay.

They want the pastor or some TV preacher to approach God for them. Oh, they know *about* God. They just don't really *know* God. Like the early Israelites in the wilderness, they refuse to draw close to God and because of this their Christian life will remain nominal.

> *This is what the LORD says: "Let not the wise man boast of his wisdom or the strong man boast of his strength or the rich man boast of his riches, but let him who boasts boast about this: that he understands and knows me, that I am the LORD, who exercises kindness, justice and righteousness on earth, for in these I delight," declares the LORD.*
> (Jeremiah 9:23-24)

Approaching the Darkness

> *When the people saw the thunder and lightning and heard the trumpet and saw the mountain in smoke, they trembled with fear. They stayed at a distance and said to Moses, "Speak to us yourself and we will listen. But do not have God speak to us or we will die." Moses said to the people, "Do not be afraid. God has come to test you, so that the fear of God will be with you to keep you from sinning."* ***The people remained at a distance, while Moses approached the thick darkness where God was.*** (Exodus 20:18-21)

The root of many people's hesitation is deeply embedded in fear. The Israelites allowed fear to rob them of the privilege of knowing God and personally hearing his voice. You see, God has placed within all of us something that is a key part of our self-defense mechanism. We just can't trust someone we don't know. The reason so many professing Christians have difficulty trusting

God is because they simply do not know God. And again, the reason they do not know God is because they are not willing to pay the required price.

God is shrouded by a thick darkness to Israelites. They can neither see nor hear him. Only a Moses will push the envelope. A Moses will dare to approach the thick darkness. A Moses will seek God and come to know him. Why? Because he will not allow fear and doubt to bar him from the privilege.

A Moses will press beyond man's self-imposed limits. He will not allow obstacles, man-made or otherwise, to stand between him and his God. He braves the heights and makes his way to the place where God resides. He then lays aside sandals that are made by man. *Man's ways, or man's skirts, are not welcome on Holy Ground.* He then is able to approach God and thus come to know him. I ask again, are you an Israelite or a Moses? Do you earnestly desire to know God? Do you ache for his presence? What price are you willing to pay for the wonderful joy of knowing our Lord? It's our ultimate calling. Yet, so many in the body of Christ settle for only a shallow, limited, relationship with God. In other words; they choose to be an Israelite rather than a Moses. Which one do you want to be?

Two of my dearest friends, Mike Powers and Ken LaDuke, were United Methodist Pastors. Some years ago, Mike was invited to a small mountain church to come and "preach a revival." One night Ken tagged alone mainly just for the ride. Upon arriving, Mike soon found himself engaged in a conversation with the pastor and some of the members. Now, this left Ken with nothing to do but to walk around the building and take in the sights.

Before I continue, it's important to tell you a little
something about my friend Ken LaDuke. Otherwise, you may
miss the humor in what transpired that evening. Ken has the
sort of personality that is easy to misjudge. His rather laid
back, soft spoken, ways don't usually inspire much excitement
when you first meet him. However, as you get to know him you
soon discover that a dry, razor-sharp, wit lies beneath that calm
exterior. When least expected, Ken can come from out of nowhere
with a remark that will have you rolling on the floor.

As Ken strolled about the interior of that small church, he
couldn't help but notice that there were multiple pictures hanging
on the walls. Upon closer observation he discovered that they
were various artists' conceptions of Jesus – *Jesus with the sheep,
Jesus knocking at the door, Jesus with the little children* and so
forth. Dozens of these framed prints, some familiar, some not so
familiar, were everywhere. They almost completely covered the
walls.

Ken was standing in the vestibule casually studying one
rather large portrait of *Jesus praying in the garden*, when he felt a
tug at his sleeve. Looking around he beheld a little old lady with a
pleasant smile staring up at him through thick glasses.

"We're glad you could come tonight, Reverend LaDuke."
she offered.

"Thank you. I'm glad I could be here." he returned.

"How do you like our pictures, Reverend LaDuke?" She
was positively beaming, obviously very proud of their collection.

"They're very nice." he said, in his usual near monotone
don't-get-me-too-excited manner. Then without missing a beat, or
offering the slightest hint of humor in his voice, he looked at her
and asked, "Who is it?"

*But whatever was to my profit I now consider loss for the sake of Christ. What is more, **I consider everything a loss compared to the surpassing greatness of knowing Christ Jesus my Lord,** for whose sake I have lost all things. I consider them rubbish, that I may gain Christ and be found in him, not having a righteousness of my own that comes from the law, but that which is through faith in Christ — the righteousness that comes from God and is by faith. I want to know Christ and the power of his resurrection and the fellowship of sharing in his sufferings, becoming like him in his death, and so, somehow, to attain to the resurrection from the dead.*

*Not that I have already obtained all this, or have already been made perfect, but I press on to take hold of that for which Christ Jesus took hold of me. Brothers, I do not consider myself yet to have taken hold of it. But one thing I do: Forgetting what is behind and straining toward what is ahead, I press on toward the goal to win the prize for which God has called me heavenward in Christ Jesus. **All of us who are mature should take such a view of things.***
(Philippians 3:7-15)

The Less Crowded Bus

*"Enter through the narrow gate. For wide is the gate and broad is the road that leads to destruction, and many enter through it. But small is the gate and narrow the road that leads to life, and **only a few find it.**"*— Jesus
(Matthew 7:13-14)

In the various crises that have occurred in the history of the church, men have come to the front that have manifested a holy recklessness that astonished their fellows. When Luther nailed his theses to the door of the cathedral at Whittenberg, cautious men were astonished at his audacity. When John Wesley ignored all church restrictions and religious propriety and preached in the fields and byways, men declared his reputation was ruined. So it has been in all ages. When the religious condition of the times called for men who were willing to sacrifice all for Christ, the demand created the supply, and there have always been found a few who were willing to be regarded reckless for the Lord. An utter recklessness concerning men's opinions and other consequences is the only attitude that can meet the needs of the present times. — Frank Bartleman (one of the fathers of the Azuza Street Revival)[98]

I reiterate; I'm just like you. I don't have all of the answers. You and I are on the same journey that the Apostle Paul was on. Like him, I started knocking down stop signs a long time ago. I'm straining toward that skirt of truth with all I have. However, also like Paul, I don't feel that I'm anywhere near there yet, but I desperately want to be!

You too, my friend, must feel the same way or you would have junked this book midway through chapter two. You're tired of religion and stand ready for a relationship. You're finished with skirt grabbing. You're through with some weak, shallow understanding of Jesus. You're ready to answer the *Mosaic Call,* to climb the mountain and approach the thick darkness where God dwells. You're finished with being one of the Israelites. You're ready to become a Moses. Am I right?

Well, come on aboard! It's a rocky ride but a *glorious* one! "What's the fare?" you ask for this bus? Well, I feel I must warn you. You will not be seated in one of those cheep economy class seats, like you'll find on all those other buses. You know... those overcrowded buses that travel around in circles. Those go-nowhere, cost-nothing, buses are always much more popular and of course much more crowded than *this* bus. You see, all the seats on this particular bus are very expensive. As a matter of fact, *a seat on this bus could cost you everything!*

"I lost it all to find everything." [99]

Spiritual Shop Lifters

When I was that lost little boy in that department store, I had only one thing on my mind—finding my mom. I would have done anything or given whatever it took to find her. No one else would do. It had to be her and *only* her! The last thing I wanted was to grab another wrong skirt!

Many of us *say* that we feel that way about Jesus. We claim that our deepest desire is to have him and only him. We say we want to know him. We say that we desire wisdom and want the One who professes to be the truth, to reveal truth to us. The only problem seems to be, however, that we're not willing to pay for the privilege. *We're a bunch of spiritual shoplifters. We want it all without having to pay for it, but it just doesn't work that way.*

Definition of a shoplifter:
Someone who tries to get something without paying for it. [100]

Many of us are laboring under a huge misconception. *We've assumed that because salvation is offered to us freely,*

the privilege of walking in a deeper revelation knowledge and
operating in manifested Holy Spirit power is also free. Yet,
nothing could be further from the truth!

With the exception of our Lord, Paul was quite possibility
the most powerful and spiritually in tuned person who ever
walked this planet. God used him like he used no other before
or since. What was Paul's secret? What was there about him that
made him such a mighty man of God?

"I want to know Christ and the power of his resurrection and
the fellowship of sharing in his sufferings, becoming like him
in his death, and so, somehow, to attain to the resurrection
from the dead."— Paul (Philippians 3:10-11)

Actually, there is no deep, dark, mysterious secret to
Paul's power. He exhibited a quality that all the great men and
women of God possessed down through the ages. His heart's cry
was, "I want to know Christ!" To know the Lord was his passion,
his life's ambition. Therefore, everything else in his life was
subject to expulsion. It mattered not to him how cherished or dear
it was to his heart. If it came between him and his desire to know
Christ, it was gone! Price was no object! If it cost him everything
he had and placed every other relationship in jeopardy, he *would*
know Christ! Only those who have crossed *this* line, those who
have boarded *this* bus, will experience the true power, authority,
and revelation that Paul and others like him did.

"Lord, send me anywhere, only go with me.
Lay any burden on me, only sustain me.
Sever any tie but the tie that binds me to thyself."
— Dr. David Livingstone's prayer[101]

What Price Obedience?

But the king (David) replied to Araunah, "No, I insist on paying you for it. ***I will not sacrifice to the LORD my God burnt offerings that cost me nothing."*** (2 Samuel 24:24)[102]

When Araunah offered his own oxen and ox yokes to King David to use for a sacrifice, David rejected it. *He knew that obedience has a price.* It requires personal sacrifice. It always has and it always will. The burnt offering *would* cost David something.

There is a price for knowing God and going on with him. That price is sacrificial obedience. Nothing less will buy passage on *this* exclusive bus. Our preconceived notions about being a Christian are just so many images hanging on the walls of our mind. They're nice and attractively framed but they're not the real thing. You'll have to discard all the skirts when you board *this* bus.

"Faith cannot be understood apart from obedience to God... The proper combination of faith and obedience can be summed up in one word: holiness. Holiness means being so full of God that there is no room for anything else."
— Dr. C. Peter Wagner[103]

O God, you are my God, earnestly I seek you;
my soul thirsts for you, my body longs for you,
in a dry and weary land where there is no water.
(Psalms 63:1)

The Gift that Keeps on Giving

I should warn you that something else is also included in the fare. In fact, it is an element that is imperative to serious Kingdom service. It is part of the price each believer must be prepared to pay if they're truly serious about having an intimate relation with God.

I began to discover in 1971 what that component is when a misunderstanding caused an unwanted breach to take place between a dear family member and myself during my time with the Navigators. This shattered relationship caused a lot of anguish for both sides and took many years to mend.

It did serve its purpose, however, by introducing me to an important new friend who gave me a very special gift. He would become a close loyal companion who remained at my side even when I was clinging to wrong skirts. The chances are that he will continue to show up in my life from time to time until I leave this world. *My friend's name is Pain. His gift to me was... brokenness.*

The sacrifices of God are a broken spirit;
a broken and contrite heart,
O God, you will not despise. (Psalms 51:17)

No pain, no gain.
Know pain, *know* gain.

God cannot use your basic self-sufficient hero-type. He has no need for a spiritual Rambo who charges into enemy territory with a blazing M-60 under each arm, *kicking rear-ends for God!* No, God desires someone very different from the world's description of a hero. God desires something of immeasurably more value, something of which he has very few. God wants broken servants. Broken servants are those who have laid aside all resistance and completely surrendered to the lordship of Christ. They have made up their minds to trust God no matter what's happening around them. They are willing to embrace brokenness while standing on God's promises; such as, "And we know that in all things God works for the good of those who love him, who have been called according to his purpose."[104]

God's hand was on my life. Brokenness was a critical element needed to fulfill my destiny. However, brokenness is a gift and, like any other gift, one must be willing to receive it.

"Earthly thrones are generally built with steps up to them; the remarkable thing about the thrones of the eternal kingdom is that the steps are all down to them. We must descend if we would reign, stoop if we would rise, gird ourselves to wash the feet of the disciples as a common slave, in order to share the royalty of our Divine Master."
— F.B. Meyer[105]

Many believers can be compared to a beautiful stallion; one that is strong, powerful, and courageous. He is an amazing creature, a marvel to behold. Wild and untamed he gallops freely like the wind. His long flowing mane blows in his wake as his magnificent coat glistens brilliantly in the sunshine. Yes, he is an extraordinary animal all right but absolutely useless until broken. Until he submits to the master, all his power, talents, and skills are absolutely useless.

Humble yourselves, therefore, under God's mighty
hand, that he may lift you up in due time.
(1 Peter 5:6)

Don't try to fix what God is trying to break.

Many of us are like that stallion. We're always running whenever the master approaches, resisting his touch and his will for our lives. But until we are willing to submit to the hand of the Master, we will be of no use to him or The Kingdom of God. Furthermore, many of us try to undo what God is trying to do in our lives that will bring us to that point of usefulness. We want to fix the very thing that God is trying to break in us. The Greek word for *humble* in 1 Peter 5:6 means *to humiliate*. Merriam-Webster defines *humiliate*, "to reduce to a lower position in one's own eyes or others' eyes."[106]

Do nothing out of selfish ambition or vain conceit, but in
humility consider others better than yourselves. Each of
you should look not only to your own interests, but also to
the interests of others. Your attitude should be the same as
that of Christ Jesus: Who, being in very nature God, did
not consider equality with God something to be grasped,
but made himself nothing, taking the very nature of a
servant, being made in human likeness. And being found
in appearance as a man, he humbled himself and became
obedient to death—even death on a cross!
(Philippians 2:3-8)

If we want to board God's bus, and finally rid ourselves of skirt grabbing, we must submit to the hand of our Master and allow brokenness to begin in us. Pride/self-centeredness is the first thing needed to be broken. We must not resist the Holy Spirit's objective no matter how painful or even how foolish it may seem to the world.

"We are fools for Christ."— Paul
(1 Corinthians 4:10)

Pride resists humiliation. Yet, that's what it takes. We must be willing to empty ourselves of all self-centered behavior, to empty ourselves of all pride. We must humiliate, or mortify, our flesh. Old fleshly attitudes are not welcome on *this* bus. It makes no difference how talented you may be, or even how many of the spiritual gifts you may display. That doesn't impress the people riding *this* bus.

Running with the Big Dogs

"The Lord has a people in these confusing times who are not confused. They are so given to Jesus, so in love with Him, so open to reproof of His Spirit, so separated from the wickedness of this age—that they know the ways and workings of the Holy Spirit. They know what is pure and holy, and what is fleshly and foolish. Whenever the cloud (of glory) moves, they follow." — David Wilkerson[107]

If you have raced with men on foot and they have worn you out, how can you compete with horses?
(Jeremiah12:5)

"Anyone can be ordinary, but a person filled with the Holy Spirit must be extraordinary."
— Smith Wiggelsworth[108]

You see, when you board this unique bus you're running with the big dogs. *Charismatic fluff, legalism, and denominational flag waving doesn't mean much to them.* Big dogs are not impressed with your noise or religious hyperactivity. *No*, not at all! That sort of foolishness doesn't exactly excite them. In fact, it has the opposite effect. *It nauseates them!*

For they know that their final destination is to be conformed to the image of Christ. And for that reason, they are attracted to the very thing that they themselves desire to see operating in their own lives and in the mist of their churches. They long for the manifestation of the character of God. They knew when they boarded that the fare would be costly for the privilege of riding on this bus. On the other hand, they also knew that the rewards would be immeasurable.

They understood that they would no longer be in a mere footrace. When they boarded *this* bus the contest shifted into a higher gear; for they stepped out of the ordinary and into the extraordinary. They are now competing with horses!

They came to realize that the fruit of the Spirit is actually evidence of the character of God in their lives. Therefore, the development of love, joy, peace, patience, kindness, goodness, faithfulness, gentleness and self-control[109] is to be desired in one's personal makeup even above gifts or even miraculous signs. Indeed, not spiritual gifts but the fruit of the Spirit *is* the sign that big dogs seek!

This attitude characterizes the passengers on this bus. Furthermore, they've come to the firm realization that without brokenness they'll never arrive at that final destination. Then sadly, God's ability to use them will be almost nonexistent. And to these big dogs the thought of being useless to their Lord is distasteful beyond words!

> *But the man who looks intently into the perfect law*
> *that gives freedom, and continues to do this,*
> *not forgetting what he has heard,* ***but doing it***
> ***-- he will be blessed in what he does.***
> (James 1:25)

10

THE WAY OF BROKENNESS

Reaching For What Is Right

*The sacrifices of God are a broken spirit; a broken
and contrite heart, O God, you will not despise.*
(Psalms 51:17)

"Who touched my clothes?" — Jesus

Mark chapter five relates an incident in the ministry of the Lord Jesus. He and his disciples were approach by a grief-stricken dad begging Jesus to come and heal his daughter who at death's door. As they were traveling to the man's home, verse five says, "A large crowd followed and pressed around [Jesus]." In the midst of the crowd, almost invisible, was a desperate lonely woman. She had been seriously ill for twelve years. "She had suffered a great deal under the care of many doctors and had spent all she had, yet instead of getting better she grew worse." (vs.26)

Jesus was seemingly unaware of her presence as she desperately tried to push her way through the unyielding throng. For years she had reached out to every resource, grabbed every skirt, but to no avail. The doctors had not healed her. He friends could not help her. Indeed, according to Mosaic Law her sickness made her unclean and an outcast of society, much like a leper. Because of her sickness she had to detach herself from all human contact. She couldn't touch anyone or anything without it becoming unclean. Therefore, she was likely deprived of the comfort of her friends and even the touch her husband.

"If I just touch his clothes, I will be healed." (vs.28)

I wonder what would have happened had she, like our little boy in the department store in the Introduction, grabbed the wrong garment. Like him she too was surrounded by a large throng of people pressing on all sides, pushing her this way and then that way. It would have been easy for her, in her weakened condition, to grab the wrong garment and be pulled further away from the Lord. Then, she would have never gotten the miracle that she so desperately longed for and, indeed, would have missed out on an encounter with the King of Kings.

Immediately her bleeding stopped and she felt in her body that she was freed from her suffering. (vs. 29)

We can learn a lot from this dear lady. She was determined to get to Jesus, grab the right garment, and be free. How many of us have that kind of resolve. How many of us are willing to push all others aside to reach our goal. Are we desperate enough that we will do anything, go anywhere, endure any anguish, drop any skirt, in order to follow Jesus? Will we dare join the big dogs on their bus?

Like the broken woman in Mark's narrative are we willing to have all the props dropped out from under us, to be so needy that we'll give up everything in order to connect with the life changing Christ? She was. Are we? The ticket for this bus is costly. For only broken servants can board this bus.

Brokenness is the difference between a treacherous deceiver named Jacob and an honorable man of God named Israel who became the father of a nation. It's the difference between a starry eyed dreamer named Joseph, and an x-con who became the Prime Minister of Egypt. Brokenness took an obscure shepherd boy named David, who was minding his father's sheep, and turned him into a king anointed to shepherd his Heavenly Father's people. Brokenness is the difference between an emotional misfit named Simon and a steady-as-a-rock apostle named Peter. It's what separates the men from the boys and the women from the girls in The Kingdom of God.

We do not want you to be uninformed, brothers, about the hardships we suffered in the province of Asia. **We were under great pressure, far beyond our ability to endure, so that we despaired even of life.** *Indeed, in our hearts we felt the sentence of death. But this happened that we might not rely on ourselves but on God, who raises the dead.*

(2 Corinthians 1:8-9)

God cannot use a self-sufficient Saul no matter how educated or zealous he may be. He needs a Paul who has weathered the storm and has allowed his will to crumble under great hardship *far beyond* his ability to endure. God needs a servant who will surrender to the process and board *this* bus. He wants a servant who will do anything, sacrifice anything, go anywhere, or undergo any struggle in order to be of service to his God and the Church.

Paul, a servant (bondslave) of Christ Jesus, called to be an apostle and set apart for the gospel of God.

(Romans 1:1)

The word "servant", or literally *bondslave,* comes from a Greek word having to do with one "who gives himself up to the will of another"[110] In ancient times *Bondslave* was the title given a free man who, after falling on hard times, would often chose to become the slave of another in order to survive. He differed in this respect from slaves who were taken in conquest or those born into slavery. *For only one who was free could become a bondslave.* Paul and other writers of the scripture knew of this common practice and often used this term to describe themselves.[111]

Paul knew that he was a free man. The work of the cross had set him free from the bondage of the law and the tyranny of sin.[112] However, he also understood the purpose of his emancipation. He would need to be free in order to qualify for the position of bondslave. Thus, having been set free by our Lord he could then, by an act of his own volition, immediately return to Christ and offer himself freely to his service as his slave—*a bondslave*.[113]

God desires to have men and women with the attitude of Paul. He wants a people who understand what it means to be called a *bondslave*. These are they who, like Job, proclaim, *"Though he slay me, yet will I hope in him."*[114] In other words, "I'm his completely. Do with me what you will no matter what it may cost." God seeks those who have yielded to the point of view that allows nothing less than a sold- out lifestyle. They have declared themselves to be bondslaves. They have given themselves up to the will of God. *Not for the purpose of getting something in return, but rather for the sole purpose of serving him whom they adore.*

This is a breed of people who walk in extraordinary power and authority. Healing is in their hands and praise is on their lips. An uncommon valor, a profound understanding of God's Word, unfeigned humility, and an unquestioning love for the lost, characterize their lives. These *sold-out saints*, these *bondslaves*, have crossed over the line, released their grips on skirts, and are determined never to turn back! Men and women who have this attitude are the ones who ride *this* bus.

> *"This is the one I esteem: he who is humble and*
> *contrite in spirit, and trembles at my word."*
> (Isaiah 66:2)

This bus is the only one that's going on with God to greater and higher things. God's manifested glory accompanies these passengers. They are his pleasure and they hold his undying respect. Yes, *the big dogs* ride this bus and they encourage you to… No, they *dare* you to come join them. Yes, the fare for boarding this bus is great, but the return is beyond measure!

Jesus Our Example

"Jesus lives in the forgotten. He has taken up residence in the ignored. He has made a mansion amidst the ill. If we want to see God, we must go among the broken and beaten and there we will see him." — Max Lucado [115]

> *Your attitude should be the same as that of Christ Jesus:*
> *Who, being in very nature God, did not consider equality*
> *with God something to be grasped, **but made himself***
> ***nothing, taking the very nature of a servant,** (bondslave)*
> *being made in human likeness. And being found in*
> *appearance as a man, he humbled himself and became*
> *obedient to death — even death on a cross!*
> (Philippians 2:5-8)

The word "humbled" used here is the same Greek word used in 1 Peter 5:6, which commands us to "*humble* ourselves under God's mighty hand." Again, one of its meanings is *to humiliate*. Are you willing to endure humiliation as part of the fare? Jesus was. As a matter of fact he was willing to obey his Father regardless of the cost even if the cost was the cross. Furthermore, he would suffer any indignity, no matter how harsh or cruel, in order to save us.

Indeed, *"he made himself nothing."* This phrase comes from a single Greek word meaning *to make empty, to abase or neutralize.*[116] In other words, our Lord emptied himself of all the rights and privileges that came with his position in The God Head. He, who was worshiped and served by myriads of angels, set aside his kingly crown. He then clothed himself with the mantle of a lowly servant, a bondslave, and surrendered his will to that of another—his Father.

Whoever claims to live in him must walk as Jesus did.
(1 John 2:6)

When you ask, you do not receive,
because you ask with wrong motives,
that you may spend what you get on your pleasures.
(James 4:3)

"You're living below your rights and privileges as a believer!" How many times have you heard this familiar battle cry from some Charismatic pulpit or some "Word of Faith" preacher? Of course this sort of *preaching* usually ends with the preacher calling on the congregation to "sow a big seed offering" into *their* particular ministry. Oh yes, you must do this in order for God to bless you and give you a big "return." What these poor, misguided saints have seemingly forgotten is that Jesus didn't redeem us and then leave us on this planet just so that we could accumulate and store-up wealth. To be certain he does bless us financially. The problem comes when we consume it on our lusts. Jesus blesses us in order for us to be able to bless others. He wants us to be a river, not a reservoir! A river continues to receive and continues to empty. Yes, Jesus wants to bless us, so that we might give it all away, in order to empty ourselves!

Then Jesus said to his disciples, "If anyone would come after me,
he must deny himself *and take up his cross and follow me."*
(Matthew 16:24)

"I have set you an example that you should do
as I have done for you."
— Jesus (John 13:15)

When we came to Christ, we agreed to walk *his* walk. In so doing, we gave up all claims to personal rights and privileges. We chose the same path that Jesus and all the great saints before us traveled. It is a path of self-denial and much sacrifice. But it is the *only* one that leads to tremendous power and anointing by the Holy Spirit.

Jesus' trail is not very busy because it's not very popular. Plus, this less traveled path can seem painfully lonely at times. It's not uncommon for one to feel somewhat alienated as they make their way. But if you look carefully around your feet you will notice something very significant. You'll see the many footprints of all those who chose to live beyond the ordinary—those who went all out for God.

Yes it's true that he is making us a kingdom of priests[117] before God and there are many wonderful benefits associated with the office. However, like our supreme example, the great High Priest,[118] we are to lay aside any rights or privileges that are normally associated with our position. Oh yes, a great day is coming when the sons of God will be revealed[119], but for now, we must walk the walk that Jesus did, the walk of a servant—*a bondslave*.

> "Jesus didn't ask people to examine his way;
> He asked them to follow it.
> He didn't ask people to debate his truth;
> He asked them to believe it.
> He didn't ask people to admire his life;
> He asked them to live it!"[120]

> *Now if we are children, then we are heirs*
> *—heirs of God and co-heirs with Christ,*
> *if indeed **we share in his sufferings in order that***
> ***we may also share in his glory.***
> (Romans 8:17)

What were some of the indignities endured by our Lord? What did he face that would serve as some examples of what we too may encounter as we get serious about serving God? What is involved in the price of a ticket on this bus? What sufferings must we be prepared to *share in* before we may *share in his glory?*

Jesus was despised and rejected by those around him.[121] He felt the pain of their rejection and wept over it.[122] He was sneered at by those who misunderstood him.[123] He was accused of insanity.[124] Even his own family joined in on this allegation and tried to put him away![125]

Yet despite rejection, opposition, and family misunderstanding, Jesus continued to press on, seeking to do God's will.[126]

Even in the mist of all the personal hurt that he endured, he still had compassion for others.[127] Finally, he suffered the worst indignity of all—betrayal and abandonment by his close friends and torture and death at the hands of his enemies. Now, are you sure that you want to share in his glory?! If so, you're ready to board *this* bus.

A Change of Clothes

Rather, clothe yourselves with the Lord Jesus Christ, and do not think about how to gratify the desires of the sinful nature.
(Romans 13:14)

That one little verse is packed with dynamite! Just for fun sometime try doing a little survey. Talk with Christians from various denominations and walks. Ask them this question. "What does it mean to be clothed with Christ?" Chances are that you'll find yourself amused and amazed. You'll be amused at the expressions on the faces of some as they try to come up with an answer to a question that they've actually never considered before.

Also, you'll be amazed at the diverse responses you'll receive. Answers will range from the sublime to the ridiculous, from the deeply profound to the childishly simplistic, from seasoned understanding to foolish prattle.

Therefore, as God's chosen people, holy and dearly loved, ***clothe yourselves*** *with compassion, kindness, humility, gentleness and patience. Bear with each other and forgive whatever grievances you may have against one another. Forgive as the Lord forgave you. And over all these virtues*

***put on** love, which binds them all together in perfect unity.
(Colossians 3:12-14)*

Simply put, to clothe oneself with the Lord Jesus is
to be, in essence, outfitted with his character. Paul elaborates
further about this when he writes to the Colossians saying to
clothe yourselves with Christ-like attributes such as compassion,
kindness, humility and so forth. In addition, Paul's phraseology
would indicate that the choice to do so is solely ours to make.
This is why he encourages us to make the right decision and
choose to clothe ourselves with these godly traits.

*And we know that in all things God works for the good of
those who love him, who have been called according to his
purpose. For those God foreknew **he also predestined to be
conformed to the likeness of his Son,** that he might be the
firstborn among many brothers.* (Romans 8:28-29)

However, be sure of this one thing. Once you've made this
choice there's no turning back. It is imperative that we be willing
to allow God full control in our lives in order for the outfitting
to commence. *He must be allowed to do whatever it takes, no
matter how uncomfortable it may seem at the time, in order to
accomplish his purpose*, which takes us back to the issue of trust.
If we truly know God, we will trust him completely. Because we
will know that what he is doing is ultimately for our benefit, for
he is molding us into the likeness of his son.

Declaring All Out War!

*I consider that our present sufferings are not worth
comparing with the glory that will be revealed in us.*
(Romans 8:18)

If we would see the character of Christ emerging in our lives; that is to see the new nature develop freely in our lives; if we would walk in power and overwhelming victory in these last days, we must declare war! War on whom? Satan and demonic powers? No, that will come after the *real* battle is won. There's a far more sinister enemy lurking in the dark recesses of our lives with whom we must first confront and defeat before we attempt to take on demonic forces!

*"If you do what is right, will you not be accepted? But if you do not do what is right, sin is crouching at your door; **it desires to have you, but you must master it**.* (Genesis 4:7)
God's warning to Cain just before he murdered his brother Abel.

Those controlled by the sinful nature cannot please God.
(Romans 8:8)

The sinful nature is the most formidable foe one will ever face! Driving Satan from our homes and our nation is a cake walk compared to the battle we face when dealing with it. We must first declare all out war on the old, earthly, nature and daily put it to death. Then and *only* then will we begin to experience the power needed to administer a death blow to influence of the forces of evil in our lives and then to share in the glory that follows.

Put to death, therefore,[seperate yourself from] whatever belongs to your earthly nature: sexual immorality, impurity, lust, evil desires [skirt grabbing]and greed, which is idolatry.
(Colossians 3:5)

Before we can put on the new nature of Christ, the old nature must suffer complete destruction. Therefore, God allows

flames of adversity to be ignited in our lives for just that purpose.
Your spirit loves it when the heat is on. In fact, it cheers it on.
Your inner spirit knows that the sinful nature is being incinerated.
The only one kicking and screaming when the heat is on is the old
nature. To it the process is very painful. Death usually is!

> *Those who belong to Christ Jesus have crucified*
> *the sinful nature with its passions and desires.*
> (Galatians 5:24)

Our spirit man knows that suffering always precedes
glory and crosses always precede a crown. There is only one
way to deal with the old flesh. You cannot negotiate, reason
with, or compromise with the sinful nature. The old man must be
terminated. Indeed, he should be annihilated!

> "There's a greater word in spiritual warfare than 'Jesus.'
> It's *'No!'*"   The best weapon you have is a righteous life."
> — Graham Cook
> (Founder of United Christian Ministries)[128]

It's a God Thing!

> *"Take **my** yoke upon you"* — Jesus
> (Matthew 11: 29)

> *"You are those **who have stood by me in my trials.** And I confer*
> *on you a kingdom, just as my Father conferred one on me, so*
> *that you may eat and drink at my table in my kingdom and sit on*
> *thrones, judging the twelve tribes of Israel."*— Jesus
> (Luke 22:28-30)

This thing we are involved in is a God thing. In other words, it's *his* mission and *his* ministry to which we are invited to join. It's *his* yoke that we are asked to take on. It's *his* trials in which we become involved. But it is also *his* kingdom that he wants to confer on us. The passengers on *this* bus have a keen perception of all this.

The Road to Greatness

for the LORD detests a perverse man but
takes the upright into his confidence.
(Proverbs 3: 32)

There is something else of phenomenal importance of which these passengers are aware. *Trust is mutual.* You see, *God will trust the one who trusts him.* He will even take him into his confidence. In fact, he will *only* work with and pour his wisdom and anointing on those who will trust him. Walking in kingdom power is *only* for those who have paid their dues and continued to place their confident in the Lord no matter what happens!

So do not throw away your confidence;
it will be richly rewarded.
(Hebrews 10: 35)

As the old hymn goes, "Trust and obey. For there's no other way to be happy in Jesus, but to trust and obey."[129] Serious God-seekers possess a rare understanding of this undeniable truth. They are therefore prepared to pay the price whatever it is, no matter how uncomfortable it makes the old nature feel, in order to get to know God intimately. *For knowing God is the key to trusting him.*

Do not be deceived: God cannot be mocked.
A man reaps what he sows.
(Galatians 6: 7)

"Call to me and I will answer you and tell you
great and unsearchable things you do not know."
(Jeremiah 33: 3)

The road to greatness in The Kingdom of God is a one way street. Indeed there is *only* one way and it's found in the principle of sowing and reaping. One reaps what one sows. If you sow seeds of doubt and mistrust, God will return to you the equivalent of what you have sown. He will not trust you. Think on it; would you divulge you innermost personal thoughts to someone who doesn't know you or trust you? Of course not!

"Whoever can be trusted with very little
can also be trusted with much..."
—Jesus (Luke 16:10)

The more effort we put into getting to really know God, the more we'll learn to trust him, the greater his willingness will be to return your trust by showing you *great and unsearchable things*. Again, it's the sowing and reaping principle. The more trust and confidence you offer God, the more he will reciprocate by opening his word to you and by filling you with the power of his Holy Spirit. It's just that simple!

Unfortunately, though, only a few professing Christians have a grasp on this great truth. Most are willing only to go just so far in their Christian walk and then they give into their sinful nature and quit. They don't submit to brokenness and getting with the program. Thus they remain nominal Christians who lead lackluster spiritual lives with little or no impact on those around them. Even worse, they will miss reaping the wonderful benefits of knowing and serving our Lord.

It's sad that so few accept the challenge to turn loose of the many wrong skirts that life has to offer and come board *this* bus. Perhaps it's merely because their desire doesn't quite match the price of the ticket!

Therefore, since we are surrounded by such a great cloud of witnesses, let us throw off everything that hinders and the sin that so easily entangles, and let us run with perseverance the race marked out for us.
(Hebrews 12: 1)

How about you? Are you ready to throw off everything —every skirt—that is holding you back from receiving Gods best for you? Are you ready to move on to a higher spiritual level? Are you serious about serving Jesus? Like Moses, are you ready to approach the thick darkness where God resides? If so, please continue reading. You've read this far and that is a good indication that you may be ready.

Still, let's do some double checking just to be sure. Do you hunger for God's presence? Do you really, I mean *really*, want to know him? Are you fed up with nominal Christianity and old stale religion? Have you decided once and for all to strive to become conformed to the image of Christ as the scripture commands? Are you willing to pay, whatever the cost, for the great privilege of boarding this particular bus?

If so, then read on. If not, and I don't mean to sound unkind, save yourself the time and effort. Find a good safe novel to read (I hear Steven King has a new one). Find someone you think is ready and give this book to them. Chances are they will benefit from it far more than you.

The Cosmic Clock

David gathered around him mighty men including men of Issachar, who understood the times and knew what Israel should do... (1 Chronicles 12:32)

I know that for some readers what I just said is a bit too hard to swallow. Some may consider me harsh, condescending, or even cruel. However, I assure you that being harsh is not my intention. I love you and don't wish to offend you. It's just that I feel emboldened to alert you to what is developing all around us.

Open your eyes and see. There's an overpowering urgency in the air! Do you sense it? Many do and they feel the same apprehension that I feel. Furthermore, I strongly sense this urgency compelling me to be direct and to the point. It's too late to worry about someone's overly sensitive feelings. I must lift my up voice in warning! *America is running out of time!*

That great cosmic clock is ticking at an exhilarated rate! Some atomic scientists created the famous Doomsday Clock.[130] It supposedly predicts how much time the world has before mankind destroys itself. According to them, as of January 14, 2010 it now stands at six minutes to midnight (the end). God has his own clock and is fervently looking for some sold-out servants in these last days. He's looking for those who are desperate to know God and to serve him. He's seeking men and women who, like the men of Issachar, understand the times and what the church should do.

Time is quickly winding down, my friend, and there's no room in this coming move of the Spirit for self-seeking, self-satisfied, denominational flag wavers. He's not looking for those who are more interested in being *politically correct,* by saying and doing things that fit into the norm, then they are in going to a higher level with God. *It's time to turn loose of those skirts!* It's time to change buses!

The Treasures of Darkness

"I will give you the treasures of darkness, riches stored in secret places, so that you may know that I am the LORD, the God of Israel, who summons you by name. "(Isaiah 45: 3)

A man reaps what he sows.
(Galatians 6: 7)

We Christians are a strange bunch! We want the treasures of darkness, those things that God alone knows. It's just that we don't want to pay anything for them. The old expression holds true. You *do* get what you pay for. You also reap in accordance with what you are *willing* to sow. If you pay nothing that is what you will get—nothing. *But, if you are willing to give your all, God will be ready to give you his all. He will reveal truths that only he and the believers on this bus know. To everyone else these truths are shrouded in darkness.*

"The growth of our church and the growth of Christianity throughout the nation of Korea did not come by accident. It came through fervent, violent, prevailing prayer."
—Dr. Paul Yonggi Cho[131]

Aside from salvation nothing in this life is free of cost. Everything has a price tag. Absolutely everything cost somebody something. This is what Dr. Cho was saying. The largest church in the world didn't suddenly just spring up in the middle of Seoul, South Korea. It was birthed and nurtured with the toil and fervent prayers of the saints living in that city. It cost Dr. Cho and his people dearly, but God honored their sacrifice and blessed them in accordance with how much they were willing to give.

Here in America, even the fading freedoms that we are fighting so desperately to hold on to aren't free. They were paid for with the blood of those who died to purchase them and also with the lives of those who gave their best to preserve them. The same holds true of the things of the spirit.

The salvation we received was offered to us free of charge, because someone else paid for it. Jesus paid for it with his own blood. The Gospel that was passed down from generation to generation and finally delivered to us was not free either. Someone else paid dearly to bring it to us. We receive it freely, because someone else gave the supreme sacrifice in order to bring it to us.

"If Jesus Christ be God and died for me, then no sacrifice
is too great for me to give for him." —C.T. Studd
(Missionary to China, India and Africa)[132]

The Open Window

*"These are the words of him who is holy and true, who holds the key of David. What he opens no one can shut, and what he shuts no one can open. I know your deeds. See, **I have placed before you an open door that no one can shut. I***

know that you have little strength, yet you have kept my word and have not denied my name."—Jesus (Revelations 3:8)

I desperately want the treasures of darkness, don't you? I crave to know the great and unsearchable things of God, don't you? I want to rid myself, once and for all, from wrong skirts, don't you? I very much want to be a part of what God is doing. Plus, I want to be a part of what he is about to do in our nation, don't you? What genuine, Holy Spirit filled, child of God doesn't?!

When N.A.S.A plans a space shuttle launch there's only so much that those involved in it can do. Once they have done all that's humanly possible in way of preparation, they are then forced to wait. They must wait for some mystical sounding factor referred to as a "launch window." This is aerospace terminology that points to that exact moment in time when everything is ready and the weather is perfect for a launch. Once the launch window is in place, they must then launch right away or miss their opportunity.

Christians in American are facing a *launch window* right now. Revival is waiting in the wings. A window, or door, of opportunity is opening right before us, but are we even ready? How many professing Christians are even capable of seeing that launch window opening? Have we prayerfully done everything humanly possible in order to be prepared for what God wants to do? If so, are we willing to sacrifice all the skirts that are holding us back from our part of God plan?

I believe that God is preparing to move across this nation in an unprecedented way. Do you want to see him do it? Better yet, do you want to be a part of it? Would you like to join in on the harvest ahead? Are you willing to pay the price of the ticket?

You are?! Well... as Tony the Tiger would say, "G-r-r-r-reat!!!" Then come along, my friend. Join me as I repent of all my skirt grabbing. Let's exchange our *death grips* for *life grips*. We can start by renouncing puny thinking, one-sided preaching, the tolerance of religious skirts, settling for the spiritual status quo, and Peter Pan skirts. Let's discard blind adherence to pet doctrines, as well as the worship of faith and the gifts.

Let us boldly break out of our self-imposed comfort zones and adopt the sanctified sentiment, "Hang the cost! I'm going for the high prize of knowing my Lord!" Let us climb on board that glory bound bus and claim our seat amid all the other righteous radicals (God bless 'em!) and then buckle up.

Listen! I do believe I hear that big ol' bus pulling up right now. We better not miss it! No telling when, or *if,* it will come our way again. Hear the hiss of the air brakes as it stops right in front of us. Look! The door is swinging wide open. You can see inside clearly now. Why... look at the driver?! I'd recognize *his* smiling face, and gentle, beckoning eyes anywhere!

I guess this is where the rubber meets the road. It's decision time! Well, I'll see you on board. I hope I do. Don't take too long. I'll try to save you a seat.

Rod Davis
Chattanooga, Tennessee

MY COMMITMENT

The following was found on a wall in the house of an African pastor who had been martyred for The Faith.

I'm a part of the fellowship of the unashamed. I have Holy Ghost power. The die has been cast. I have stepped over the line. The decision has been made. I'm a disciple of His. I won't look back, let up, slow down, back up or be still.

My past is redeemed. My present makes sense. My future is secure. I'm finished and done with low living, sight walking, small planning, smooth knees, colorless dreams, tamed visions, mundane talking, cheap living and dwarfed goals.

I no longer need preeminence, prosperity, positions, promotions, plaudits or popularity. I don't have to be right, first, tops, recognized, praised, regarded, or rewarded. I now live by faith, lean on His presence, walk by patience, lift by prayer, and labor by power.

My face is set, my gait is fast, my goal is heaven, my road is narrow, my way rough, my companions few, my Guide reliable, my mission clear. I cannot be bought, compromised, detoured, lured away, turned back, deluded or delayed. I will not flinch in the face of sacrifice, hesitate in the presence of the adversary, negotiate at the table of the enemy, ponder at the pool of popularity or meander in the maze of mediocrity.

I won't give up, shut up, let up, until I have stayed up, stored up, prayed up, paid up, preached up for the cause of Christ. I am a disciple of Jesus. I must go till He comes, give till I drop, preach till all know and work till He stops me. And when He comes for His own, He will have no problem recognizing me—my banner will be clear! [133]

ENDNOTES

1   John 14: 8-9

2   Matthew 7:21

3   Vs. 23

4   *Living Life Upside Down* by Russ Lee | from the album
Pictures On Mantles: The Best Of Russ Lee

5   "Of the three major religious societies of Judaism at the
time of the New Testament (the Pharisees, the Sadducees,
and the Essenes), the Pharisees were often the most vocal and
influential." "The name Pharisee in its Hebrew form means
separatists, or the separated ones. They were also known
as chasidim, which means loyal to God, or loved of God -
extremely ironic in view of the fact that by His time, they
made themselves the most bitter, and deadly, opponents of
Jesus Christ and His message." *Retrieved from the Daily Bible
Study* by Wayne Blank at *www.keyway.ca*

"During the time of Christ and the New Testament era,
the Sadducees were aristocrats. They tended to be wealthy
and held powerful positions, including that of chief priests
and high priest, and they held the majority of the 70 seats of
the ruling council called the Sanhedrin. They worked hard to
keep the peace by agreeing with the decisions of Rome (Israel
at this time was under Roman control), and they seemed to
be more concerned with politics than religion. Because they
were accommodating to Rome and were the wealthy upper
class, they did not relate well to the common man, nor did
the common man hold them in high opinion. The common
man related better to those who belonged to the party of the
Pharisees. Though the Sadducees held the majority of seats
in the Sanhedrin, history indicates that much of the time
they had to go along with the ideas of the Pharisaic minority,
because the Pharisees were popular with the masses." Taken
from *www.gotquestions.org - Bible Questions Answered* ©
Copyright 2002-2010 Got Questions Ministries - All Rights
Reserved. *Retrieved on October, 10, 2010*

6   John 8:26

7   Vs.3

8   The Greek word is "metanoeo". It literally means to perceive afterwards, hence it signifies to change one's mind or purpose, and it always involves a change for the better. *Vine's Expository Dictionary of New Testament Words* W.E. Vine M.A., Copyright (C) 1985, Thomas Nelson Publishers

9   The word "gospel" means to announce good news. It's good news that we don't have to be enslaved by sin and eventually end up in Hell. For Jesus' death, burial, and resurrection made a way for us to be free from sin's bondage and destruction. Jesus gave his life in order to become the door to a life free of guilt and condemnation. We not only have Heaven to look forward to, we can now to be friends with God.

"For God so loved the world that he gave his one and only Son, that whoever believes in him shall not perish but have eternal life. For God did not send his Son into the world to condemn the world, but to save the world through him. Whoever believes in him is not condemned, but whoever does not believe stands condemned already because he has not believed in the name of God's one and only Son." — Jesus (John 3:16-18)

10   A metaphor for a list of the names of all of those who made a real commitment to Jesus

11   Pentecost is historically and symbolically related to the Jewish harvest festival of Shavuot, which commemorates God giving the Ten Commandments at Mount Sinai fifty days after the Exodus. Among Christians, Pentecost commemorates the descent of the Holy Spirit upon the Apostles and other followers of Jesus as described in the New Testament Acts of the Apostles 2:1-31. For this reason, Pentecost is sometimes described as the "Birthday of the Church". (Taken from the *Wikimedia Foundation at http://wikimediafoundation.org Retrieved on May, 2, 2009*

12   Acts chapter 2

13   Ephesians 3:20

14   Luke 19:10

15   Taken from *Christian Quote of the Day* — Copyright 1999-
2003. *Retrieved April 26, 2004, from http://cqod.gospelcom.net/*

16   Taken from *Christian Quote of the Day* — Copyright 1999-
2003. *Retrieved April 26, 2004, from http://cqod.gospelcom.net/*

17   Taken from *http://abcnews.go.com/print?id=2914953 on
September 10, 2010* Copyright © 2010 ABC News Internet
Ventures

18   My apologies to Tommy Flanagan (a.k.a. Jon Lovitz)

19   Taken from *The Barna Group, Ltd* — Copyright © 1995-
2004. Retrieved on April 22, 2003, from http://www.barna.
org/

20   Taken from *WorldofQuotes.com*, All the Rest © 2003-2010
Roy Russo. All rights reserved Retrieved on march 8, 2008

21   Taken from *Merriam-Webster Dictionary* © 2010 Merriam-
Webster Retrieved on June 5, 2009

22   The island of Patmos is today part of Greece. It is located
among the Sporades group of islands in The Aegean Sea
near the west coast of Turkey. It is a relatively small member
of the group, measuring only about 6 by 10 miles / 10 by 16
kilometers, with a very irregular coastline. Taken from *Daily
Bible Study* by Wayne Blank at *www.keyway.ca*. *Retrieved on
July, 7, 2010*

23   *I Won't Grow Up* from the Album Peter Pan, words and
music by Rickie Lee Jones Artist - Peter Pan soundtrack from
the Album - Peter Pan

24   *Power BibleCD* is Copyright 2003 by Online Publishing,
Inc.

25   *I Shall Not Be Moved* Words & music by Homer Morris,
copyright unknown

26   Hebrews 12:29

27   *The New Strong's Exhaustive Concordance of the Bible*, by James Strong Thomas Nelson Publishers (1991)

28   Taken from David's official website, copyright unknown — *http://www.forgivenforlife.com/parole.htm Retrieved on October 23, 2008*

29   *Holy Bible, The New Living Translation* Copyright © 1996 by Tyndale House Publishers.

30   *In The Presence of a Holy God* by Mark Altrogge © 1988 Integrity's Praise! Music/People of Destiny Music/BMI Integrity's Praise! Music

31   Stated on his TV program *The Potter's House*

32   *We Bring The Sacrifice Of Praise* - Written By: Kirk Dearman - © 1984

33   1 Samuel 15:22

34   "And if any place will not welcome you or listen to you, shake the dust off your feet when you leave, as a testimony against them." — Jesus (Mark 6:11)

35   *The New Testament: An Expanded Translation.* Kenneth S. Wuest, Grand Rapids: Eerdmans, 1961. Reprinted 1994. Wm. B. Eerdmans Publishing Co.; (June 1984)

36   Taken from *Bible Study Tools at http://www.biblestudytools. com/* Copyright © 2010, Bible Study Tools. All rights reserved. Article Images Copyright © 2010 JupiterImages Corporation.

37   *Word Studies in the Greek New Testament*, Kenneth S. Wuest, Grand Rapids: Eerdmans, 1961. Reprinted 1994. Wm. B. Eerdmans Publishing Co.; (June 1984)

38   Matthew 12:25

39   Taken from *BrainyQuote.* — Copyright 2004 BrainyMedia.com *http://www.brainyquote.com Retrieved on April 27, 2004*

40   My dear friend Roy Cantrell is pastor of City Gate
Church in Chattanooga, TN

41   There are different kinds of gifts, but the same Spirit.
There are different kinds of service, but the same Lord. There
are different kinds of working, but the same God works
all of them in all men. Now to each one the manifestation
of the Spirit is given for the common good. To one there is
given through the Spirit the message of wisdom, to another
the message of knowledge by means of the same Spirit, to
another faith by the same Spirit, to another gifts of healing
by that one Spirit, to another miraculous powers, to another
prophecy, to another distinguishing between spirits, to another
speaking in different kinds of tongues, and to still another
the interpretation of tongues. All these are the work of one
and the same Spirit, and he gives them to each one, just as he
determines. (1Corinthians 12:4-11 NIV)

42   Acts 1:8

43   *The New Testament: An Expanded Translation*, Kenneth S.
Wuest, Grand Rapids: Eerdmans, 1961. Reprinted 1994. Wm.
B. Eerdmans Publishing Co.; (June 1984)

44   Luke 24:49

45   1Corinthians 14:2

46   *Vine's Expository Dictionary of New Testament Words* W.E.
Vine M.A., Copyright (C) 1985, Thomas Nelson Publishers

47   Then Jesus came from Galilee to the Jordan to be
baptized by John. But John tried to deter him, saying, "I need
to be baptized by you, and do you come to me?" Jesus replied,
"Let it be so now; it is proper for us to do this to fulfill all
righteousness." Then John consented. As soon as Jesus was
baptized, he went up out of the water. At that moment heaven
was opened, and he saw the Spirit of God descending like
a dove and lighting on him. And a voice from heaven said,
"This is my Son, whom I love; with him I am well pleased."
(Matthew 3:13-17)

48   Matthew 3:17

49   Acts 19:6

50   Acts 4:31

51   Romans 14:4 and 13

52   Galatians 5:6

53   John 13:35

54   1Corinthians.14:39

55   Vine, W. E.; Unger, Merrill F.; White, William: *Vine's Complete Expository Dictionary of Old and New Testament Words.* Nashville : T. Nelson, 1996, S. 2:381

56   Phileo is to be distinguished from agapao in this, that phileo more nearly represents "tender affection". *(Vine's)* Jesus didn't command us to have "tender affection" toward one another. God will not demand our feelings but he will demand our obedience to practice love toward others.

57   In New Testament times a talent was worth more than $1000. In USA, in today's market, five talents of silver or gold would today be worth from $2,880,000 - $4,320,000

58   *When the Morning Comes* Words & Music by Charles A. Tindley, 1905

59   Peter 3:21

60   Psalms 118:24

61   Ephesians 2:8-9

62   John 13:34

63   John 13:35

64   Clara Peller (August 4, 1902 – August 11, 1987), was a retired manicurist and American character actress who, at the age of 81, starred in the 1984 "Where's The Beef?" advertising campaign for the Wendy's fast food restaurant chain,

created by the Dancer Fitzgerald Sample ad agency. Taken from *wikipedia.org, http://en.wikipedia.org/wiki/Where%27s_the_beef%3F.* Text is available under the Creative Commons Attribution-ShareAlike License; additional terms may apply. See Terms of Use for details. Wikipedia® is a registered trademark of the Wikimedia Foundation, Inc., a non-profit organization.

65   Believer's Voice of Victory, TBN 01/20/91 Taken from *Apprising Ministries at http://apprising.org/2008/08/25/john-avanzini-word-faith-wolf-and-prosperity-preacher/ Retrieved on September 20, 2010*

66   Believer's Voice of Victory program on TBN (January 20, 1991). *Taken from The Bible Page http://www.thebiblepage.org/avoid/avanzini.shtml http://www.brainyquote.com. Retrieved on September 20, 2010*

67   I'm relating this account from memory. To be fair I don't remember verbatim everything Mr. Avanzini said that day. However, I do remember the theme of his words and have tried to present it as accurately as possible and have even inserted quotes taken from John Avanzini's blog at *http://johnavanzini.wordpress.com/* that support my recollection. *Retrieved on September 20, 2010*

68   Proverbs 11:24, 25 KJV

69   Malachi 3:8-11 KJV

70   *Success in Life,* May 12, 2004, The Word Network. "In 1991, Diane Sawyer and ABC News conducted an investigation of Tilton (as well as two other Dallas-area televangelists, W.V. Grant and Larry Lea). The investigation, assisted by Trinity Foundation president Ole Anthony and broadcast on ABC's Primetime Live on November 21, 1991, found that Tilton's ministry threw away prayer requests without reading them, keeping only the accompanying money or valuables sent to the ministry by viewers, garnering his ministry an estimated US $80 million a year. Ole Anthony, a Dallas-based minister whose Trinity Foundation church works with the homeless and the poor on the east side of Dallas, took an interest in Tilton's ministry after some of the

people coming to the Trinity Foundation for help told him
they had lost all of their money making donations to some of
the higher profile televangelists, especially fellow Dallas-area
minister Robert Tilton." Taken from *http://en.wikipedia.org/wiki/*
Robert_Tilton#Exploitation_of_vulnerable_people on 10/01/10.
Text is available under the Creative Commons Attribution-
ShareAlike License; additional terms may apply. See Terms
of Use for details. Wikipedia® is a registered trademark of
the Wikimedia Foundation, Inc., a non-profit organization.
Retrieved on September 19, 2010

71   Psalm 37:25

72   Creflo Dollar Crusade, February 9, 1999

73   *The Hundredfold Promise can be Yours!* Benny Hinn
Ministries E-NewsLetter August 17, 2007

74   *Claim Your Miracles* (audiotape #186, side 2)

75   *Ever Increasing Faith* (TBN December 9, 1990)

76   For more information on the Azusa Street Revival go to
http://en.wikipedia.org/wiki/Azusa_Street_Revival#Beliefs

77   For more on the Jesus Movement go to *http://en.wikipedia.*
org/wiki/Jesus_movement#Origins

78   *Engaging the Enemy,* by C. Peter Wagner. (Ventura, CA:
Regal Books, 1991)

79   Matthew 5:14

80   Romans 8:37

81   Psalms 46:1

82   Colossians 3:1

83   Source: Merrill D. Peterson, ed., Jefferson Writings, (New
York: Literary Classics of the United States, Inc., 1984), Vol.
IV, p. 289. From *Jefferson's Notes on the State of Virginia,* Query
XVIII, 1781.

84   "America's moral decline rapidly accelerated following one event — the U.S. Supreme Court's removal of prayer from our nation's schools. On June 25, 1962, 39 million students were forbidden to do what they and their predecessors had been doing since the founding of our nation – publicly calling upon the name of the Lord at the beginning of each school day." Taken from *Banning Prayer in Public Schools Has Led to America's Demise* by Gary Bergel. Published May 1988. *Retrieved on October, 2, 2010* (To read the entire article go to *http://www.forerunner.com/forerunner/X0098_Ban_on_school_prayer.html*)

85   Ruth Graham, wife of Evangelist Billy Graham, was credited with saying this.

86   *Old Time Religion*, Words & Music: Anonymous

87   *Vine's Expository Dictionary of New Testament Words* W.E. Vine M.A., Copyright (C) 1985, Thomas Nelson Publishers

88   A Zonies are someone who are passionate about the old TV show The Twilight Zone.

89   Read Numbers chapter 13 and 14

90   *Experiencing God* by Henry T. Blackaby and Claude V. King. Compiled by Trent Butler. ©1995 by Broadman & Holman Publishers

91   Taken from *BrainyQuote* — © 2010 BrainyMedia.com. *Retrieved on February 8, 2010, from http://www.brainyquote.com*

92   John 11

93   Luke 10:19

94   Source Unknown

95   Source Unknown

96   For more information about Buford Pusser go to *http://en.wikipedia.org/wiki/Buford_Pusser*

97   *The New Strong's Exhaustive Concordance of the Bible,* by James Strong, Thomas Nelson Publishers (1991)

98   *Another Wave of Revival* by Frank Bartleman, Whitaker house. © 1962

99   *I Lost It All To Find Everything* - Composed by: William J. Gaither, Gloria Gaither and Carol McMillen © 1976

100   This definition is my own.

101   Taken from *Christian Quote of the Day* — Copyright 1999-2003. *Retrieved April 25, 2004, from http://cqod.gospelcom.net/ Retrieved on September 19, 2009*

102   Read 2 Samuel chapter 24 to see the reason for David's sacrifice

103   Romans 8:28

104   Romans 8:28

105   *Taken from http://cqod.gospelcom.net/, Christian Quote of the Day* — Copyright 1999-2003. *Retrieved on May 2, 2004*

106   *© 2010 Merriam-Webster,* Incorporated

107   *Seven Women Shall Lay Hold of One Man!* A message from David Wilkerson, posted on the Times Square Church Pulpit Series September 18, 1995. *Retrieved May 1, 2004, from http:// www.tscpulpitseries.org/english/1990s/ts950918.html*

108   *Smith Wigglesworth Apostle of Faith* by Stanley Frodsham, Harrison House, Incorporated; (1982)

109   Galatians 5:22

110   *Vine's Expository Dictionary of New Testament Words* W.E. Vine M.A., Copyright (C) 1985, Thomas Nelson Publishers

111   Romans 1:1, 1 Cor. 9:19, Gal. 1:10, Titus 1:1, James 1:1, 2 Pet. 1:1, Jude 1, Rev. 1:1

112   Romans 8:1-4

113   Romans 6:15-23, 1 Cor. 7:22

114   Job 13:15

115   Taken from *Christian Quote of the Day* — Copyright 1999-2003. Retrieved May 6, 2004, from http://cqod.gospelcom.net/

116   *The New Strong's Exhaustive Concordance of the Bible,* **by** James Strong, Thomas. Nelson Publishers (1991)

117   Revelation 1:5 and 5:10

118   Hebrews 8

119   Romans 8:19

120   Source unknown

121   Isaiah 53:3, John 1:11, John 5:43

122   Matthew 23:37

123   Luke 16:14

124   John 10:20

125   Mark 3:21

126   Mark 14:36

127   Luke 19:41

128   I heard him say this at a conference some years ago.

129   *Trust and Obey* words by John H. Sammis. Music by Daniel B. Towner, 1887.

130   The Doomsday Clock is a symbolic clock face, maintained since 1947 by the board of directors of the Bulletin of the Atomic Scientists at the University of Chicago.

The closer the clock is to midnight, the closer the world is estimated to be to global disaster. As of January 14, 2010, the Doomsday Clock now stands at six minutes to midnight. Since its creation, the time on the clock has changed 19 times.

Originally, the analogy represented the threat of global nuclear war, but since 2007 it has also reflected climate-changing technologies and "new developments in the life sciences and nanotechnology that could inflict irrevocable harm." Copyright (C) 2010 Permission is granted to copy, distribute and/or modify this document under the terms of the GNU Free Documentation License, Version 1.3 or any later version published by the Free Software Foundation; with no Invariant Sections, no Front-Cover Texts, and no Back-Cover Texts. A copy of the license is included in the section entitled "GNU Free Documentation License". *This page was last modified on 28 February 2010 at 05:16. http://en.wikipedia.org/wiki/ Doomsday_Clock*

Text is available under the Creative Commons Attribution-ShareAlike License; additional terms may apply. See Terms of Use for details. Wikipedia® is a registered trademark of the Wikimedia Foundation, Inc., a non-profit organization.

[The major problem I see with the Doomsday Clock is that these so-called scientists do not take into account that God has his own clock. The cosmos will be destroyed until God says that it's time. "No one knows about that day or hour, not even the angels in heaven, nor the Son, but only the Father." –Jesus, Mark 13:32]

131   Taken from *BrainyQuote* — © 2010 BrainyMedia.com. *Retrieved on April 27,2004, from http://www.brainyquote.com.* (Dr. Cho is Senior Pastor and founder of the Yoido Full Gospel Church (Assemblies of God), the world's largest congregation with a membership of 830,000 (as of 2007)

132   Taken from *Christian Quote of the Day* — Copyright 1999-2003. *Retrieved May 26, 2004, from http://cqod.gospelcom.net/*

133   Source unknown

ABOUT THE AUTHOR...

From his military days in the Signal Corp, during the Vietnam era, to his three decades on radio, 'Rappin' Rod Davis has been a communicator; an on-air voice of support to those in need of direction. His humor, insight and inspiration has echoed in the kitchens, the cars, and iPods of spiritual seekers for the better part of three generations. His voice has likewise reverberated from pulpits, concert stages and inner city sidewalks throughout the South.

The father of three and grandfather of three, Rod Davis is the president and founder of Soaring Wings Ministries and serves as Chaplain Emeritus for Partners for Christian Media/J103 Radio in his hometown of Chattanooga, Tennessee.

THE REVIEWS ARE IN...

Reading The Wrong Skirt, was fun, insightful, and right on target. Rod has captured the essence of today's search for meaningful faith and hope for the future. As a pastor for over 30 years I have seen firsthand the struggles people go through; the foolish choices they make in their search for truth. Rod Davis has clearly described this struggle and given a beautiful plan for choosing the right path for one's life. I hope that many will read and apply this book to their lives.

Terry and Lynn Davis, Retired Senior Pastor
Serving Ocean City Baptist Church, Ocean City, MD for 31 years
www.ocbaptist.com , www.occalm.com

THE WRONG SKIRT
THE QUEST TO AVOID BAD CHOICES

ISBN978-1-935434-55-9

ROD DAVIS